FROM
A-TRAIN
TO
YOGI

FROM A-TRAIN TO YOGI

The Fan's Book of Sports Nicknames

Chuck Wielgus and Alexander Wolff
with Steve Rushin

A SMITH & KRAUS INC. BOOK

PERENNIAL LIBRARY

HARPER & ROW, PUBLISHERS, New York
Cambridge, Philadelphia, San Francisco, Washington
London, Mexico City, São Paulo, Singapore, Sydney

A Smith & Kraus Inc. Book

FIRST EDITION

Copy editor: Stephanie Grant

Library of Congress Cataloging-in-Publication Data

Wielgus, Chuck.
  From A-Train to Yogi.

  1. Sports—Miscellanea. 2. Athletic clubs—United States—Names. 3. Athletes—
United States—Names. I. Wolff, Alexander, 1957–. II. Rushin, Steve. III. Title.
GV706.8.W53 1987   796   87–45085
ISBN 0–06–096163–5 (pbk.)

88 89 90 91 HC 10 9 8 7 6 5 4 3 2 1

For
Irene and Charles,
Mary and Nikolaus,
and Jane and Don,
whose nicknames are Mom and Dad

Acknowledgments

In producing this book, the authors drew on broadcast and published sources too numerous to name, or even nickname. We would, however, like to mention by formal name a few living and breathing sources whose contributions were special. They include Jason Bickler, Mark Bradley, Bob Brown, Brooks Clark, Tim Hanlon, Henry Hecht, Mike Hodan, Roger Jackson, Todd Larson, Franz Lidz, Jack McCartan, Mike McCollow, Ivan Maisel, Craig Masback, Merrell Noden, Keith Opatz, Charlie Pierce, Andrew Ramsay, Jim Rushin, Bob Sullivan, Julie Vader, Mike Villafana and Steve Wulf.

Preface

The beginning of wisdom is to call things by their right names.

—Old Chinese proverb

This much we knew from the very start: That the one southpaw in the crowd was called Lefty. The one redhead, Red. And every fat kid was called Bubba.

Nicknames and sport. Have two things ever been more perfectly suited to one another? We hardly limit ourselves in tagging with affectionate names the elements in our athletic universe. It doesn't stop with people. Places like The Launching Pad and The Dome on the Range get nicknames, too. So do events; the Thrilla in Manila begat the Rumble in the Jungle, which begat the Drama in Bahama. (Without Ali, alas, these wonderful rhymelets are becoming more and more scarce.) The Super Bowl took its name from Kansas City Chiefs owner Lamar Hunt, who noticed his kid playing with a high-bouncing rubber orb, all the rage in the late 1960s, called a Super Ball. But we nickname much more: teams, units, mascots, broadcasters and legions of fans, from Arnie's Army to Tway's Twoops. Even the sporting world's softshoes—everything from the Sack Dance to the Boris Boogie—have cognomens they can call their own.

In bestowing and using nicknames, we want something very specific in return. It's not accuracy, necessarily. That Mordecai (Three Finger) Brown really had four digits on the hand in question is not a matter of particular concern. That we know why Dennis Boyd goes by Oil Can, however, *is.*

Sports nicknames take as inspiration many disparate sources. In the developing nation of Zimbabwe, for instance, a fascination with technology might well have led to a certain boxer taking the ring name Jukebox Timebomb. For some athletes, like Lou (The Toe) Groza, we look to synecdoche. For others, like Walt (No Neck) Williams, we look instead to a sort of synecdoche *manqué.* (Still others, like the NFL's Bills, look punningly to other cities in New York State.)

History showered us with nicknames long before big-time spectator sport began keeping us happily in nickname slop. Among her French peasant constituency, Marie Antoinette was known as L'Autrichienne—the Austrian bitch—while members of Parliament were so inured to his windy ramblings that they up and went off to eat whenever Edmund (Dinnerbell) Burke rose to speak. And could there really have been such a big difference between Ivan the Terrible and Alexander the Great other than in how adept the flacks of each were at spin control?

U.S. presidents, from John (His Rotundity) Adams, to John (His Accidency) Tyler, to Rutherford B. (His Fraudulency) Hayes, have merited a long line of respectful sobriquets. Dwight (Ike) Eisenhower installed a resolute chief of staff, Sherman (The Abominable No-Man) Adams. Those depressed by the policies of Franklin (The New Dealer) Roosevelt called FDR, among other things, The Raw Dealer, Kangaroosevelt and A Traitor to His Class. (Give 'Em Hell) Harry Truman had nothing on John Kennedy, who decreed to the press that he was *never* to be known as Jack. But the most appropriate presidential nickname belonged to Richard (Tricky Dick) Nixon. In college, years before he had it kicked out of office, he was known as Iron Butt. That's almost as earthy as Betty Ford's CB radio handle, First Mama.

Popular music has supplied us with Frank (The Chairman of the Board) Sinatra, Bing (Der Bingle) Crosby, Jerry (The Iceman) Butler, James (The Godfather of Soul) Brown and Bruce (The Boss) Springsteen. (In a denotative sense, the Boss isn't so terribly different from the Chairman of the Board.) We can thank jazz and blues for such names as Charlie (Bird) Parker, McKinley (Muddy Waters) Morganfield, Ferdinand (Jelly Roll) Morton and Louis (Satchmo) Armstrong. Satchmo is a contraction of "satchel mouth," which isn't quite as regal as Count Basie or Duke Ellington, but reflects the unsparing ability nicknames have for getting things just right.

Most of these artists earned nicknames that reflected a career's worth of reverence and respect. As sports fans, we can be a little tougher on occasion. But, for the most part, we go about the business of manufacturing monikers because we want intimacy with our heroes. We want to immerse ourselves in the subculture of sport, and nicknames help us do that. But nicknames are also reminiscent of the schoolyard, where shorthand, saucy appellations first arose in the primal soup of our banter and teasing and insecurities. Using nicknames helps us return to childhood on a small, possible scale. So we conspire, usually as mythologizers and sometimes as put-down artists, to conjure up alternative ways to refer to athletes. To have something to call 'em for short.

For short. Throughout sport there's a prevailing spirit of truncation, an ethic of less is more. Sports abbreviations, rather than circumscribing that for which they stand, enhance: the cadence of "MVP" has a ring of importance that "Most Valuable Player" can't approach. Similarly, 99 percent of all Mets fans couldn't tell you that their team's official name is "The New York Metropolitan Baseball Club," but they'd love to excommunicate the one percent who do. Good nicknames serve this spirit of encoded informality. Consider Earvin (Magic) Johnson. Magic and Earvin are both words of two syllables, but while the latter only denotes, the former does that *and* connotes—a pass, a smile, a moment.

Sports fans often read a shortened broadsheet called a tabloid, which is known, for short, as a tab, which happens also to be a short, slang verb (a sort of *nick* verb, in a sense) meaning *to name.* That verb is often found *in* tabs as part of headlines. TAB MAGIC NBA MVP may read to many like a banner in a beverage-trade journal, but to those party to the clannish code of sport, it sings.

Indeed, nicknames help us establish a family outside our own. Through them, strangers become familiar—and familial. The only field that approaches sport for the frequency and color of its nicknames is that most familial of realms, organized crime. "In 1936 the FBI announced that it had collected more than 100,000 'criminal nicknames' in a special moniker file," Paul Dickson writes in *Names.* "These were nicknames, not aliases. As J. Edgar Hoover later explained, aliases changed all the time but nicknames stuck. Because the nicknames were often based on appearance, mannerisms, or attitudes, they were considered valuable clues." Valuable clues, indeed. It wouldn't be too difficult to pick Fred (No Nose) Delucia out of a police lineup. (Eat 'Em Up) Jack McManus, Vincent (Mad Dog) Coll and Nathan (Kid Dropper) Kaplan might prove a little trickier to identify, as would Jack (Machine Gun) McGurn, who wasn't to be confused with fellow thug George (Machine Gun) Kelly—or with (Machine Gun) Lou Butera, the billiards player who carried his cue in a violin case. Joe Valachi deserves a Tony award for his 1963 testimony before the McClellan Committee, in which he spilled the beans about nine different colleagues named

Anthony. How to keep 'em all straight? Let's see—there was Tough Tony, Little Tony, Fat Tony, Tony Boy, Tony the Bum, Tony the Sheik, Tony Cheese, Tony Bananas and Tony the Geep.

Far too often, nicknames come out of the typewriters of sportswriters who are striving for some sort of cheap immortality. That's where the Tom Terrifics and Galloping Ghosts come from. But the best nicknames are thumbnail character sketches that at once encapsulate and enhance. In fact, etymologists tell us that *nickname* is derived from the Old English *eke name,* out of the verb *ecan,* meaning to augment. Yet *nickname* is also a misnomer of sorts, because a felicitous nickname doesn't "nick" its subject, but nails it, gets it just right, gouges a little piece of that person—or place or event or whatever—with its edge of accuracy and correctness. Phooey to those who claim that a nickname is fluff, superfluous p.r. or self-aggrandizement. "Those who have no nicknames have no social existence," says Rom Harre, a professor at Oxford. "They are non-people. It may be better to be called Sewage than merely John."

We've approached this book less as a reference work than as a reader, with nicknames serving as jumping-off points for stories. We chose entries based on the quality and richness of the nickname rather than the fame of the nicknamee. As is so often the case in sports, one yarn will lead to another, and another, and another, off to wherever the raconteur in each of us decides to go. That's because, above all, nicknames evoke. For the fan, they evoke memories, joyous and painful. For the athlete, they're a brand of his achievements and limitations, usually birthed in action. Any number of athletes actually nickname themselves, but even those who don't can—through their performances—have some say in what they're called.

More say, at least, than in whatever's on their birth certificates.

(Ground) Chuck Wielgus
Alexander (The Grate) Wolff
Steve (White) Rushin

FROM
A-TRAIN
TO
YOGI

TAGS AS TITLES

Ever notice how many legendary coaches just happen to have nick-names fit for, well, for a legendary coach? *Bear* Bryant. *Doc* Counsil-man. *Pop* Warner. It's as if, when each was but a wee lad, the Nickname God took up their cases right after having devoured a couple of Chip Hilton novels. This rule doesn't hold universally, of course. Connie Mack doesn't have quite the dignity that Cornelius McGillicuddy does. But don't ever let anyone tell you that nicknames are necessarily disre-spectful.

Sonny (The Drummer Boy) Liston . . . because of the bongo beating he gave opponents. When Liston wanted another card at Las Vegas blackjack tables, he would stick an index finger in the air, eye the dealer and say, "One for the Drummer Boy." Then again, would any dealer have responded if the former heavyweight champion of the world had uttered the customary "Hit me"?

Jim (Three Ninety-five) Brosnan . . . because his novel, *The Long Season,* cost that much when he received this (price) tag in 1961—a year in which his earned-run average was 91 cents lower than his nickname.

Oail Andrews (Bum) Phillips . . . because nobody in this NFL coach's family could pronounce Oail, and a sister's attempt at saying "brother" came out "bumble." Phillips doesn't mind the moniker, "As long as you don't put a 'you' in front of it."

1

Lyman (Smiley) Quick . . . because this great amateur of the 1940s had a winning grin. He so liked his sobriquet that he legally traded in Lyman for Smiley.

TAKIN' IT TO THE STREETS

A toast. Cheers to these three boulevardiers, sport's men about town:

(Jefferson St.) Joe Gilliam. This quarterback had anti-freeze in his veins at Tennessee State, where he was named for one of Nashville's main arteries.

(Rush St.) Reggie Theus. On State Street, that great street . . . so what did Sinatra know? Reggie T., the *GQ* dude who put the *Chic* in Chicago, knew where Chi-town was *really* toddlin' after Bulls' games. He dropped the nickname after being deported, via Kansas City, to Sacramento, where folks have yet to hear him sing "My Kind of Town."

(Broadway) Joe Namath. For his brash repartee, not to mention his love of a good partee. Joe Willie's willy-nilly training regimen often found him on The Great White Way, where he would later perform on stage.

TABLE LABELS

Frank (Spoon) James . . . for reasons almost nobody knows, and this former U. of Nevada, Las Vegas (UNLV) basketball player refuses as a matter of principle to reveal. (They are not, he insists, drug-related.) A roommate once overheard Spoon in a phone conversation with his grandmother. "You know why, and I know why," he told Grandma, "but I'm not tellin' aaaaaaanybody else." Nor is he telling why brother Karl James is called Boobie. Naa-naa-na-naa-naa.

Thomas (Pepper) Johnson . . . because he was fond of peppering his cereal as a youth. (He has since outgrown that practice, and now reserves pepper for such foods as apple pie.)

Spious (Spice) Kilpatrick . . . because that's how they garbled his first name at New York City's Madison Square Boy's Club, where it takes a 'pious man to follow Jeff (Monkey Jesus) Shepherd (see page 144). Spice also hung out with Ken (Mouse) McFadden (see page 27) at the MSBC.

BERMANTICS

You can tell a fair amount about ESPN SportsCenter anchor Chris Berman from the marvelous nicknames he comes up with to flavor his nightly narrations of baseball highlights on the all-sports cable network. He likes movies: Jose (Blame It on) Rijo; Tim (Purple) Raines; John (Private) Tudor; and continental cuisine: (Fettuccini) Alfredo Griffin. He keeps abreast of world affairs: Brian (10) Downing (Street); Julio (Generalissimo) Franco. He's a wise consumer: Joe (Actual Retail) Price; Billy (Free) Sample, whose tastes sometimes run expensive; Jerry (Rolls) Reuss; Mike (Izod) LaCoss; Larry (Satin) Sheets. What else is a kid to do when he has that early Bert (Be Home) Blyleven curfew? It isn't beneath Berman to plug his employer, Nino ESPNosa, nor is he above waxing philosophical, Oddibe (Young Again) McDowell.

You hardly need a philosophical bent to fashion some of the schtick-names Berman specializes in. Rather, you just need to *be* bent. Berman unstraightened himself at Brown, where neither friends nor professors were spared his punmanship. When he joined ESPN as a sort of Brat Packer, the network was in its salad days—pass the Butch (Oil and) Wynegar—all fresh and sassy, ready to try anything. So Berman dropped a few nicknames on a graveyard shift broadcast of SportsCenter. Viewer response was so overwhelming that he unleashed his act during prime time. "Sports isn't brain surgery," Berman says. "Let's have some fun with it." O.K. His personal favorite? Rick (The Innocent) Lysander.

When a humorless higher-up briefly put the kibosh on Berman's creative sallies at the end of the 1985 season, he responded by putting an embargo on all nicknames, as a sort of protest. A couple of broadcasts filled with references to St. Louis Cardinals manager Dorrel Herzog brought things back to normal, as did an uprising of Bermaniacs across the country, including Kansas City third-baseman George Brett. As much as Brett enjoys the nicknames, he's just as furious that Berman hasn't nicknamed him yet.

Until such time, Brett is calling the nickname man Chris (Ethel) Berman.

THE BEST OF CHRIS BERMAN

Berman's Hermits: Nicknames of Note

Manny (Kingston) Trillo
Jody Davis (Eyes)
Daryl (Please Come to) Boston
Wally (Takin' Care of Business) Backman
Kirby (Union Gap) Puckett
Jamie (Men at) Quirk
Joel (C'mon People Now) Youngblood
Ross (I Never Promised You a) Baumgarten
Jose (Won't You Take Me on a Sea) Cruz
Ron (Born in the U.S.) Cey
Greg (Crocodile) Brock
Von (Purple) Hayes
Cliff (Brothers) Johnson
Bob (Ebony Eyes) Welch
Glenn (Surfin' U.S.A.) Wilson
Bill (Doran) Doran
Ruppert (Along Came) Jones
Bob Melvin (and the Blue Notes)
Danny (Uriah) Heep
Don Aase (/DC)
Frank (101 Strings) Viola
(Me and) Willie McGee

John (Pass the) Grubb: Food and Drink

John (Clams) Castino
Dave (Prince) Righetti
Tom (Cotton) Candiotti

Bruce (Eggs) Benedict
Wade (Cranberry) Boggs
Mike Heath (Bar)
Bill (Toasted) Almon
Henry Cotto (Salami)
Julio Franco (-American)

. . . and from the Jim (Singles) Barr:

Frank Tanana (Daiquiri)
Tony Pena (Colada)
Mario (Scotch and) Soto
Doyle (Brandy) Alexander
Dave (Vodka) Collins
Jeff (Wine) Sellers

Rick (Really Big) Schuh: TV and the Movies

Tom (Leave It to) Seaver
John Mayberry (RFD)
Jerry (Rowan and) Martin
Jay (Thurston B.) Howell
Paul Moskau (on the Hudson)
Pete (Maltese) Falcone
Geoff (Wrath of) Zahn
Ken (Magnum) Forsch
Jeff (Romancing the) Stone
Jeff Dedmon (Don't Wear Plaid)
Tommy (Ben) Herr
Bill (Hello) Dawley
Scott (Tallulah) Bankhead
Mike (Perry) Mason
Jeff Lahti (Dah)
Bob (Laverne and) Shirley
Ken (Good Evening, Mister) Phelps

. . . and for the commercial break:

John (Tonight, Let It Be) Lowenstein

AND FOR GOOD MEASURE:

Mark (Beetle) Bailey
Bob (The Car, Please) James
Reid (Buffalo) Nichols
Mike (Great) Scott
Chris (Church) Speier
Glenn (Mr. Outside) Davis
Bob (Yom) Kipper
Jose (Mother) Guzman
Reuben (High) Sierra
Art (And) Howe
Victor Mata (Hari)
Jerry (The World Is My) Royster
Joe (The Autobiography of Miss Jane) Pittman
Gary Redus (A Bedtime Story)
Jamie Easterly (Winds)
Bruce Kison (Make Up)
Charlie Puleo (Vaccine)
Vern (The Golden) Ruhle
Ron (Greco-) Romanick
Ray (I Dub Thee) Knight
Rob (Rein) Deer

Byron (Whizzer) White . . . because of the speed with which this All-American and Rhodes Scholar gave up his football career for a seat on the bench. Upon his appointment to the Supreme Court by JFK, White became the first and quite possibly last Whizzer among the Brethren.

Winfrey (Wimp) Sanderson . . . because, as this Alabama basketball coach himself tells it, "I was named Winfrey after my mother's brother, who blocked a punt and died shortly thereafter"; and because Uncle Winfrey's nephew's sister couldn't pronounce Winfrey, and came up with Wimp.

Clyde (Pea Ridge) Day . . . because this early-day Dodger hailed from Pea Ridge, Ark., where he was best known for calling hogs. After Day

would "K" a batter, he'd cup his hand to his mouth and squeal trium-
phantly, "Soooooo-eeeeee!"

ANSWERING A KNEED

Word spread pretty quickly around the Southeastern Massachusetts
University campus when Juvan (Torn) Cartledge ripped two rims from
their moorings in Tripp Gym one fine winter's day in 1986. It spread
first to the basketball office, where Juvan's 6'7", 215-pound dimensions
were duly registered by coach Brian Baptiste, as was the fact that Juvan
wasn't on the team roster. Seems that Cartledge's sport-of-choice at
Boston's Hyde Park High had been swimming. Where he was no doubt
known as Juvan (Floating) Cartledge.

WEE, THE PEOPLE

Norwood (Pee Wee) Barber . . . because it beats the alternative. As
his coach at Florida State, Pat Kennedy, says: "If *your* name were
Norwood, *you'd* want to be called Pee Wee, too."

(Wee) Willie Keeler . . . because he was a small Bill of great value,
whose trenchant hitting philosophy doubled as his other nickname: Hit
'Em, Where They Ain't.

Harold (Pee Wee) Reese . . . because "I was the marbles champion
of Louisville, and Pee Wee was my shooter. I didn't use an immie. I
used a pee wee."

NAME THAT D

When the Cincinnati Bengals had the NFL's top-rated defense in 1983, linebacker Reggie Williams figured it was time they got a nickname. *The Cincinnati Enquirer* asked its readers to do the honors, and the response was overwhelming. Overwhelmingly bad. One suggestion was Carnivore Roar, a nickname that inspired one Bengal to ask, "What's a carnivore?" That same player probably puzzled over submissions like A Knockwork Orange and Pumpkin Patch Kids. Stars in Stripes, Black and Orange Crunching Machine, Banzai Bunch and the pithy River Bend Butt Busters didn't catch on, either. The winner? The Pittsburgh Steelers, in the opener, setting a tone that would eventually make the question academic.

The Nickname-the-Defense contest naturally reached new heights in the Mile-High City in 1984. There, 10,380 entries were submitted to the *Rocky Mountain News,* which had decided that The Orange Crush was passé. Denver Broncos fans knew the import of their task. One woman wrote, "If there is anything I can do to bribe the judges, let me know." She submitted The Strip Teasers.

Alas, the winner was Plundering Herd. The judges knocked Opportuni-D, The Habitual Defenders, Mothers of Smother, Rulon Jones and the Temple of Doom and The No-Hole-in-the-Wall Gang. Runners-up were Joe's Bait and Tackle and The Pillage People. Other entries ranged from the pointless (Pointus Interruptus) to the classical (Symphony in D Major).

Cleveland once billed its defense as The Browns' Bombers, taking off on boxer Joe (The Brown Bomber) Louis. Why not The Broncs' Bombers in Denver? The entire discussion makes The Orange Crush sound pretty good, as the *News* would find out. Considering Denver's D over many of these years, The Soda Jerks wouldn't have been half bad, either.

Leo (The Lip) Durocher . . . because of this infielder and manager's garrulous nature. His garish couture as a Yankee rookie also earned him the appellation Fifth Avenue.

Fort Landry . . . because of the hermetic security and military regimen Tom Landry maintains at the Dallas Cowboys training/boot camp in Thousand Oaks, California.

Maureen (Goldflinger) Flowers . . . because this blond Brit was the top female dart thrower in the world.

Hugh (Losing Pitcher) Mulcahy . . . because he lost seventy-six games in four of his seasons in Philadelphia. From 1937 to 1940, the newspaper summaries of most of his games carried this line at the bottom: *Losing Pitcher—Mulcahy.* In today's box score vernacular, he'd just be "LP."

Dave (Elmer) Concepcion . . . because Larry Bowa once asked him, one shortstop to another: "Is your first name Elmer?" When the puzzled Concepcion asked why, Bowa replied, "Because every time I look in the box score, I see 'E-Concepcion.'" Pete Rose calls Elmer the more-flattering Bozo, because his suits only come in two colors, checks and plaid.

Paul (Boo Boo) Palmer, Temple's star tailback, on his moniker: "It's a cute nickname given to a cute kid by the great-grandmother who raised him from the time he was three years old."

HIGH SCHOOL HIJINKS

Gimme an S! Gimme an O! Gimme a C! Gimme a K! Gimme another S! Whatsatspell? The name of teams from Argyll Academy, a prep school in California.

Change came slowly in Illinois, where Pekin High had been piquing Chinese-Americans ever since the 1930s, when their teams were called the Chinks. In 1980 the school grudgingly became the Dragons, after the student council decided in favor of dragging itself into the twentieth century.

When it comes to creative nicknaming in high school athletics, rural schools seem to rule the roost. Brush, Colo. has its Beet Diggers; the Haybalers pitch for Hollister (Calif.) High; Texas has Cotton Pickers (from Robstown) and Fighting Farmers (from Lewisville); the Tillamook (Ore.) Cheesemakers are only occasionally creamed and the Hoopeston-East Lynn (Ill.) Corn Jerkers . . . well, to headline writers they're a bunch of Jerks.

What right-thinking team of fencers would schedule a duel with the Bad Axe (Mich.) Hatchets? Who wants to wrestle the Red Elephants of Gainesville (Ga.) High? Those Effingham (Ill.) Flaming Hearts are no doubt pretty easy pickin's on the football field.

In 1910, Yuma High School in Arizona was temporarily housed above the Yuma Prison, thus sentencing its teams to life as the Criminals.

One school without such a checkered past is Poca (W.Va.) High. Their teams are called the Dots.

Yuma High School (Criminals)

SPACE CADETS

Greg (The Reno Rocket) LeMond . . . because of this Nevada native's expeditious expeditions by bicycle. Had he not taken up cycling (and taken the Tour de France title from Bernard [The Badger] Hinault in 1986), LeMond might have made quite a name for himself in hoops: His last name is misspelled French for "The World."

DeWayne (Astronaut) Scales . . . because of his anti-gravitational feats of derring-DeW, one of which he described thusly: "I just got me an Astronaut dunk and drummed it home." Indeed, drummed it home with earthshaking force that would befit a DeWayne (Richter) Scales.

The Launching Pad . . . because of the frequency with which home runs are hit in Atlanta–Fulton County Stadium. With its treacherous soil making it a diamond in the rough, the stadium's infield is called The Rock Pile.

ABC'S

Even before the Jackson 5 became The Jacksons, the group that crooned "ABC" knew the ABC's of creating a new image—or reinforcing an old one—by changing a name. In sports, the old switcheroo is the truest show of devotion to a nickname, and it *is* easy as A–B–C. Altered Birth Certificates are still a relative rarity in sport, though more and more athletes who resent being called something other than their ego-massaging nicknames are making court dates. Approval is seldom denied those looking to make the legal leap.

Boxer Marvin Hagler has always considered himself marvelous in the ring, and those who saw him make Thomas (Hitman) Hearns a Hit-the-Canvas-Man would probably concur. But it wasn't until 1982 that describing this middleweight champ as marvelous became officially redundant. That's when he changed his name in Plymouth (Mass.)

Probate Court from Marvin Nathaniel Hagler to *Marvelous Marvin Hagler.* And no, he isn't Marv, not even to his friends.

While growing up in the Brownsville section of Brooklyn, Lloyd Free was accorded All-World status on the basketball court. "Anybody who was anybody in Brownsville had a nickname," says Free, whose own moniker had metamorphosed from "Twirl" (a reference to his deft 360s) to "World." "We already had a Kangaroo Kid and a Helicopter, so All-Mayberry Street wouldn't have sounded like much," says Free. Once again, life imitated the art of nicknames, this time with a flair typical of the Prince of Midair. In 1982, Lloyd became *World B. Free,* incorporating his nickname into a legal name that still smacked of its playground roots. It even has a philosophical ring to it, although by World's own admission, "The B. stands for nothin'."

Mark Duper has had more name changes than a typical episode of *Dragnet.* When Walter Dupas entered the Army, a misguided typist recorded his name as Duper. He gave his son Mark the name Dupas, but the child eventually got tied up in the runaway red tape and began answering to Duper. In high school and college in Louisiana, Mark's superlative speed and hands earned him a nickname that nicely complemented the clerical snafu: *Super.* In 1985, the Miami Dolphin made a quick trip to Dade County (Fla.) Court, where Mark Kirby Dupas was christened anew. "It's no big deal," insisted *Mark Super Duper.* "I just decided to have my name changed. I could have changed it to Jack Nicholson if I wanted." A–B–C. A shining example of how easy it can be.

Frederick Koch was having a more difficult time. Everyone knew how to pronounce his son Bill's name—after all, *he* was a silver-medalist cross-country skier in the 1980 Olympics, where his name had been correctly pronounced "coke" by countless broadcasters. Father Frederick, however, often had his name mispronounced "Kotch," and he was getting tired of correcting people. In 1985, after a settlement with the Coca-Cola Company, he had his name legally changed to *Frederick Coke-Is-It.* Still another example of a nickname becoming the real thing.

Howie (Caveman) Long . . . because, though Darwin overlooked this fact in *The Origin of Species,* this lineman on a goal-line stand falls somewhere between Neanderthal and Cro-Magnon on the evolutionary scale.

Mark (Super) Duper

Jack (Mount) Morris . . . because this pitcher had his volcanic ash kicked badly during one slump, and subsequently blew his top at umpires with the nerve to call his close pitches balls.

Barry (The Last) Word . . . because of the finality with which this tailback ran at the University of Virginia, where he was nicknamed, and named Atlantic Coast Conference Player of the Year for 1985.

Dave (Double O) Bristol . . . because "He makes so many bed checks," one of his players in Cincinnati once said, "it's like having Agent 007 around."

RAILSIDE RHUBARB

So, who was the *real* Big Red, Man o' War or Secretariat? (No votes for Cornell, please.) Man o' War certainly had the requisite large frame and red chestnut color first. But Secretariat's groom, Ed Sweat, started calling his charge Big Red at age three. Though Secretariat evoked comparisons to Man o' War, purists were appalled. Secretariat did have a few fallback monikers: Ol' Hopalong (so tagged as a two-year-old, for his clumsy gait during workouts); Sexy; and the absolute trump card of a tag, *Super* Red.

Willie (Mookie) Wilson . . . because this outfielder's family, watching him growing up in South Carolina, noticed how the word "milk" came out when he tried pronouncing it.

Louis (Hot) Lipps . . . because this fleet receiver made a string of sensational catches when he joined the Pittsburgh Steelers, forcing him to kiss goodbye *Sweet,* the a.k.a. he had earned at Southern Mississippi.

Gene (The Machine) Littler . . . because of his effortless, classic swing.

Bob (Death to Flying Things) Ferguson . . . because he was a sterling fielder during the nineteenth century, a gilded age for nicknames. Ferguson could really pick it, but he was *not* immortal, as those who have erroneously called him Bob (Death-Defying Thing) Ferguson would have you believe.

VIRGIN STEEL

Like the virgin birth, the Immaculate Reception required a little help from above. Sure, when Franco Harris crossed the goal line with five seconds left in that 1972 playoff game he gave the Pittsburgh Steelers a 13–7 win over the Oakland Raiders. But nobody was quite sure if Terry Bradshaw's pass had deflected off Raider safety Jack (The Assassin) Tatum or Steeler receiver John (Frenchy) Fuqua before bouncing back seven yards and being saved inches from the Three Rivers Stadium carpet by Harris, who carried it forty-two yards for the apparent TD.

Referee Fred Swearingen was pretty sure the ball had hit *Tatum* at the 35, and therefore was caught legally by Harris. Tatum, though, could've sworn it hit Fuqua. That's when The Man Upstairs phoned the field, requesting to speak to the ref. (Actually, it was NFL Supervisor of Officials Art McNally, calling from the press box.) "How do you rule?" McNally asked. Swearingen tried, "Touchdown." Replied McNally, who had just watched the replay, "You're right." The call stood.

If the Reception was Immaculate, it was also Accidental. Bradshaw was supposed to throw to Barry Pearson, who couldn't get open. So he looked instead to Fuqua. "I saw the ball and thought I could catch it, but I felt someone [Tatum] hit me from behind," spoke Frenchy. "Next thing I knew, Franco went roaring past me and I wondered what the hell was going on."

To hear the Immaculate Receiver tell it, the play probably should have been remembered by its humbler, original designation—the one in all the papers the next day: Pitt—Harris, 60 pass from Bradshaw (Gerela kick).

Indeed, it was anything but Immaculate to Franco. "I wasn't even supposed to be out there," he said. "I thought Terry was in trouble, having to scramble, so I better get out there if he had to throw to me. But he threw it deep."

But you caught it anyway. The Immaculate Reception.

"Sure," said Harris. "I was damn lucky."

ITEMS FROM OUR MENU

⚾ **Frank (Taters) Lary** . . . because not only did he surrender a few taters in his time, but this pitcher from Northport, Ala. also once wrote that word, and nothing else, on a dining-car order blank.

🏀 **Anthony (Spud) Webb** . . . because, as a kid, the head on the NBA's only 5'6" slam-dunk champ seemed as big as the Soviet satellite *Sputnik* that had just been launched. "Sputnik" became "Spud," though pro

Anthony (Spud) Webb

basketball's original Tater Tot has never felt compelled to comply with the law of gravity.

Jim (Cakes) Palmer . . . because this pitcher attributed a shutout he pitched as a nineteen-year-old to a breakfast of pancakes. This was long before he began doing beefcake ads for men's underwear.

Julio (Juice) Cruz . . . because Seattle Mariners teammate Juan Bernhardt was having difficulty addressing Cruz while the two were strolling through a shopping mall. "He was from the Dominican Republic and couldn't pronounce my name," says Cruz. "I said, 'Hey, I'm Spanish. It's *Hoolio.*'" Bernhardt was still struggling when he spotted an Orange Julius stand and decided, "I'll just call you Juice."

O.J. (The Juice) Simpson . . . because folklore had it that his initials stood for Orange Juice. This delightful fiction led to Simpson's offensive line in Buffalo being dubbed The Electric Company, "for springing loose the juice." Alas, the O is for Orenthal, the J for James.

Helen (Muffin) Spencer-Devlin . . . because the forceps marks imbedded on her forehead as a newborn suggested a freshly baked muffin.

Elvis (Toast) Patterson . . . because this New York Giants cornerback is always getting burned.

Willie (Chicken on the Hill Will) Stargell . . . because Stargell's restaurant in Pittsburgh's Hill District offered free chicken whenever the owner homered. His more universal nickname is Pops, after his role as patriarch of the Pirate Fam-i-lee that won the 1979 World Series.

Melvin (The Great Pumpkin) Turpin . . . because of this Cleveland Cavalier's orbicular appearance in his orange road uniform. As a collegian at Kentucky, Turpin was known as The Dipper for an appetite so prodigious that coach Joe B. Hall assigned a student manager to maintain 'round-the-clock surveillance of this ravenous 'Cat. When a sympathetic sort smuggled some chocolate chip cookies into the Wildcat Lodge dormitory, Turpin upbraided him. "How many times do I have to say it?" he said. "Ya don't feed the Dipper!"

Helen (Muffin) Spencer-Devlin

CORNBREAD

Cedric Maxwell became Cornbread after he and his friends checked out *Cornbread, Earl and Me.* You don't remember it? "He's the man with a plan, got a basketball in his hand," went the film's title song. "He's Corrrrrn-breeeaad." Set in a ghetto, this forgettable black exploitation flick starred Keith Wilkes as the ball-toting Cornbread. Young Cedric's pals decided that Wilkes, a former Laker whose first name is now Jamaal and whose nickname has always been Silk, looked just like Maxwell. Though he was born and bred Cedric, Max was Corn and Bread through his days at the University of North Carolina, Charlotte and his first few seasons with the Celtics, after which he requested that the nickname be put to rest. It should be noted here that Maxwell and Wilkes look *nothing* alike.

Chris (The Tin Man) Brown . . . because the Padres' third baseman was alleged to have no heart. (Perhaps he should see Cards' shortstop Ozzie [The Wizard of Oz] Smith.) The Atlanta Hawks' Jon Koncak took the same rap—and nickname—as a collegian at SMU.

John (The Count) Montefusco . . . because of his name's resemblance to the title of Alexandre Dumas's novel *The Count of Monte Cristo.* Edmond Dantes, the fictional Count, pitched battles while Montefusco pitched batting practice, but the difference didn't seem to matter until Montefusco moved to New York, where the media had other nickname notions. Inasmuch as the Yankees had acquired him to solve their righthanded pitching woes, Montefusco was heralded as the Great Right Hope.

Nat (Sweetwater) Clifton . . . because this former Globetrotter, who helped integrate the NBA with the Knicks, "was always drinking sweetwater," as a ladyfriend of his says. Are we to take that to mean wine? "Oh, no. He was always drinking Pepsi or other kinds of pop. But when that wasn't around, he'd mix sugar with water and drink it."

Steve (The Kid) Cauthen . . . because this precocious jockey broke in as a seventeen-year-old. The question of what happens to such a nickname when a Kid grows up needn't concern us; it's a problem for the British, whom Cauthen has spent his post-teens racing for.

THE BABE

You have to go back to George Washington to find an American who has spawned as large a body of lore as George Herman Ruth. The Father of our Country didn't *really* chop down that cherry tree and 'fess up to his dad. As much as we'd like to believe that story to be true, it isn't—and neither are these tales about the origin of Ruth's nickname:

- Young Georgie yearned so badly to play baseball with the big kids on the Baltimore streets that he'd wail when they wouldn't let him. "Baby," they called him, and the Babe bit his lip and vowed to become the greatest player of all time.
- On his first trip in the minor leagues, Ruth stuck his head out of an ascending hotel elevator, damn near getting decapitated. "You're just a babe in the woods," said the kindly old veteran who literally saved the rookie's neck.

By Ruth's own account, the event was considerably less dramatic. When Baltimore manager Jack Dunn brought his new prospect into the Orioles clubhouse for the first time, "some guy named Steinam," as Ruth would recall, said, "Here comes Dunnie with his newest babe." Some Guy Named Steinam had created a household name. (So what if the guy's name was Sam *Steinman*.)

The Babe was American in a way that George Herman somehow wasn't. Many Japanese soldiers in World War II spoke only five words of English: "To hell with Babe Ruth!" Italian immigrants didn't have to speak the language to address their new hero immediately. They called him the *bambino*. The Bambino. The Babe. Ruth begat nicknames like no one else in sports.

To his teammates he was Jedge, because that's how catcher Benny Bengough once mangled Ruth's given name. To the writers, he was The Sultan of Swat. The Babe himself had a terrible time with names, and called most veterans Doc. All the others were Kid. For three seasons, Ruth's bat had a nickname—Black Betsy.

He was Babe Ruth of Murderers' Row of the Bronx Bombers, who

(The Babe)

made the journey from St. Mary's Industrial School where he grew up, to the big leagues; from The Home—as St. Mary's was called in Baltimore—to The House That Ruth Built—as Yankee Stadium was first called by sportswriter Fred Lieb. From Dunnie's babe in 1914 to *the* Babe forever after.

Babe Ruth's Legs . . . because Sammy Byrd was the languorous legend's defensive replacement. Baseball historian Bill James knows of no other nickname quite like this. Says he, "No one was ever called Mark Belanger's bat."

LETTERMEN

Terry (L. D.) Williams . . . because, in the words of this SMU forward, "it's a long distance from my head to my toes."

Lawrence (L. T.) Taylor . . . because, in this All-Pro linebacker's case, initials are quite adequate. Besides, it has the sound of a conquistador, à la El Cid, of which Taylor is a gridiron version.

Ken (K. T.) Landreaux . . . because this outfielder made it up. "People make up names all the time," he says. "Look at the scientists. Who tells them water is H_2O?"

Ernie (Ernie D) DeGregorio . . . because it's much easier to say than his full seven-syllable name. When, as a pro, Ernie showed that he didn't give a one-syllable word about defense, he became Ernie (No) D.

DOG TAGS . . .

Albert (Sparky) Lyle . . . because "My parents thought they were gonna have a dog."

Bill (Doggie) Dawley . . . because, one spring training, this pitcher wore a Pluto hat that he bought at Disney World.

Jim (Dog) Gantner . . . because of the new life he breathed into the oldest of clichés. "Never bother a sleeping dog," he warned. "He might bite."

Bill (Mad Dog) Madlock . . . because the Wrigley Field Bleacher Bums who so nicknamed him enjoy alliteration. Mad Dog said those Chicago Cubs fans called him that "with affection." Madlock lost his froth when he moved to Pittsburgh, and was licensed as Pet Hound by his brethren there. A trade from the lowly Pirates to the contending Dodgers brought Madlock half-circle, from Mad Dog to Glad Dog.

. . . AND OTHER PET NAMES

René (Le Crocodil) LaCoste . . . because this Gallic tastemaker-to-be played a positively snappy brand of tennis. In 1933, he began wearing a small crocodile patch on his polo shirts, and in 1951 named his *chemises* for English tailor Jack Izod and began marketing them. The Crocodile has been known forever after for his "alligator shirt." Yeah, we know there's a difference.

Ken (Snake) Stabler . . . because of the serpentine route this future quarterback, who grew up on Alabama's Redneck Riviera, took while returning a punt for a touchdown in a junior varsity high school game. "Damn," his coach was moved to say, "that boy runs like a snake."

Harvey (The Kitten) Haddix . . . because of the likeness this long-faced pitcher bore to Harry (The Cat) Breechen.

Jim (Mudcat) Grant . . . because his mother was always having to call him up to the house from his favorite fishing hole in Lacoochie, Fla.

Walt (Moose) Dropo . . . because Moosup, Connecticut was once his mailing address.

Kevin (The Beaver) Houston . . . because of this slightly built Army guard's resemblance to actor Jerry Mathers. Houston was such a pro-lific scorer, in fact, that Cadets coach Les Wothke, trying to impress the rest of his team with how little they were contributing, once accused them of "playing 'Leave It to Beaver.' "

Ken (The Rat) Linseman . . . because of this miniature Broad Street Bully's reputation for being a cheap shot DaVinci. Flyers teammate Bobby Clarke was inspired to play *Name That Goon,* and Linseman insists he has never much liked the resulting nickname. So why do you have a rat tattoo on your right calf, Kenny?

Marty (The Octopus) Marion . . . because this dexterous shortstop showed such remarkable range afield that he seemed to have surplus hands.

Jack (The Golden Bear) Nicklaus . . . because of his blond hair and ample build. If he hadn't won a few tournaments along the way, he might still be known as Ohio Fats or Baby Beef, the latter courtesy Bob Hope. Nicklaus certainly has given Golden Bear a pinstriped profile, what with his Golden Bear line of clothing, and chairmanship of Golden Bear, Inc. (As befits someone of such a magnificent moniker, his entry immediately precedes "nickname" in the *Encyclopedia Americana.*)

Dave (The Cobra) Parker . . . because of this slugger's venomous strikes at opposing pitchers. Parker calls his home run trot *The Thing.*

THE NICKNAME THAT FIRED DON ZIMMER

The nickname didn't exactly barrel into Don (The Gerbil) Zimmer's office and cry, "Clean out your desk!" It worked more subtly than that. Nevertheless, says Zimmer, his nickname as manager of the Boston Red Sox *did* cost him his job there. The four steps, from sobriquet to severance pay:

Verbal Abuse. Before the 1978 season, two Sox pitchers are traded. Zimmer tells reporters how happy he is now that "we don't have anybody like Rick Wise and Fergie Jenkins, who cried all the time, got the hell beat out of them and blamed me."

Gerbil Abuse. On behalf of the deposed pitchers, the Bosox' Bill

(Spaceman) Lee says that Zimmer looks like a gerbil—which instantly becomes the manager's new nickname. One member of the Gerbil litter, minor league manager Tom Zimmer, is branded Gerbil Junior. The nickname fosters disrespect and ridicule in the Boston clubhouse, Zimmer argues, leaving him with little authority. "I guess I should have apologized," Lee would say later. "To the gerbils."

Buffalo Quip. From his new home in Texas, Jenkins suggests that Zimmer's nickname should really be Buffalo. "A buffalo is the dumbest animal on earth," he says.

Fergie Gets Hip. Following the 1980 season, the Gerbil is fired in Boston. When it becomes apparent that he'll become Texas' new manager, a penitent Jenkins, still a Ranger, insists: "*Zimmy* and I have patched it all up."

The Possum Brothers . . . because these two Cardinals pitchers, roomies Danny Cox and Kurt Kepshire, "sleep all day and run all night," according to trainer Gene Geiselmann. "You could grow mushrooms in their room. The shades are always down."

Jerry (Tark the Shark) Tarkanian . . . because of the UNLV coach's knack for procuring talent. The Shark survived swimmingly in the desert, where fans at Runnin' Rebels games form ersatz shark jaws with their hands and the band plays the theme from *Jaws.*

John (Guppy) Troup . . . because the team he bowled with as a youth was called The Guppies.

James (Fly) Williams . . . because this Brooklyn playground legend never flinched at letting the ball do just that. At Austin Peay, the crowd was fond of chanting, "The Fly is open! Let's go Peay!"

Livingstone (Pit Bull) Bramble . . . because of the pedigree of his dog Snake. This former lightweight champ was long called Donna, after the hurricane that slammed into the West Indies when he was born there in 1960. Nowadays he prefers Pit Bull—or Livingstone, we presume.

James (Fly) Williams

Karl (The Albino Rhino) Mecklenburg . . . because this Broncos linebacker is white and charges often. So why wasn't he nicknamed Valley Girl?

Walter (The Greyhound) Davis . . . because he's lithe, *not* because he's big and slow and rarely on time. Otherwise, for years the Phoenix Suns would have had a gas-guzzling offense that saw a Greyhound and a Truck (Len Robinson) running side by side.

Ken (Mouse) McFadden . . . because this star Cleveland State guard, whom Viking fans paid homage to by leaving mousetraps outside his dorm room, has a friend named Cat.

Mary (The Bunny) Bacon . . . because of the Lady Godiva-like, if not altogether ladylike, pictures this jockey posed for in *Playboy* magazine. As one shrewd handicapper would suggest, Bacon could always be counted on to "show."

Jim (Hippo) Vaughan . . . because, as one of this old-timer's former teammates has reminisced, "Compared to the Refrigerator, he was a walk-in meat locker."

HOW COME NONE'S CALLED "WOODY"?

The first known bat nickname was handed out in 1884, when Pete Browning of the Louisville Eclipse rapped three hits with a stick sculpted for him by one Bud Hillerich. Hillerich & Bradsby have been branding "Louisville Slugger" on their bats ever since.

The century to follow has featured Roy *(The Natural)* Hobbs, fictional hero of the Bernard Malamud novel and Robert Redford flick, wield his magical Wonderboy; and the *science*-fictional flake Jay Johnstone swing with his Business Partner. Babe Ruth never considered parting with his Black Betsy, the bat he credited for some torrid slugging. In Baltimore fifty years later, Al Bumbry would also swing a black bat. But in the wake of black power, dashikis and *Roots,* Bumbry dubbed his The Soul Pole.

⚾ **Walt (No Neck) Williams** . . . because he can't wear a necklace, because he's neckless.

🏀 **Spencer (Driftwood) Haywood** . . . because this great forward made the trans-Atlantic float to European basketball when his NBA career began to rot.

🏈 **The Crunch Berries** . . . because Kansas defensive backs Tony Berry and Derek Berry hit so hard.

⚾ **Larry (Larry) Cox** . . . because he looks like Larry Fine of Three Stooges fame. A teammate once introduced Cox to a friend thusly: "His name is Larry, but everyone just calls him Larry."

O'S & D'S

By definition, *The Lawrence Welk Offense* has never been employed with success. Though many football teams still use it, the result is always the same: Uh one and uh two and uh three and uh kick.

At the University of Texas, coach Fred Akers was equally unsuccessful with his defense in the Longhorns' 55–17 loss to Iowa in the 1984 Freedom Bowl. Following that game, critics spoke of the 'Horns' installing a *Highway Patrol Defense,* to keep opponents under fifty-five.

In getting to the 1987 Final Four, Providence relied on a full-court press that assistant coach Gordie Chiesa called the *Mother-in-Law Defense* for its "constant pressure and harassment."

The Los Angeles Lakers have long been fond of fast-breaking with the basketball, yet when jump-shooter Bob McAdoo was with the team, he could be counted on to break up that dull routine by sticking a shot off the half-court offense. He was, you could say, a Hardy proponent of the team's *Sean Cassidy Offense,* in which the play-by-play sheet always seemed to read "McAdoo, Run, Run, Run . . ."

Other basketball teams for whom defense is not a primary concern have employed an *Anne Murray Offense*. Their members are always cheating on defense to get a head start on the fast break. In hoopspeak, they're looking to *Snowbird*.

HEADY BALLPLAYERS

Joe (Steeplehead) Ward . . . because this former Georgia and Athletes-in-Action star had the spirit—and an absolutely spic-and-span head. Fellow born-again athlete Willie Gault, at whose wedding Ward officiated, also noted how it came to a point.

Gilberto (Onionhead) Reyes . . . because of the shape of his head. (The Athenian statesman Pericles was nicknamed *Schinocephalus,* or Onionhead, some 2,500 years before Reyes would toil in the Cubs' farm system. Like Reyes at the plate, Pericles usually wore a helmet to hide the inspiration for his nickname.)

HEADLINES

The inspiration for Doug (The Pea-Headed Giant) Adkins's nickname sat within this Chicago Bear's ball-bearing-sized helmet. Former Providence basketballer Aubrey (The Antman) Stallworth was also heavy-set and of *petite tête*. Likewise Bill Cartwright, the Knick center who's built like the TransAmerica Building—with a wide base that tapers off toward the top. His Euclidean bod begs the nickname The Human Isosceles Triangle.

W.C. HANDLES

Tommy (Mascara) Nunez . . . because this NBA referee is said to lead the league in make-up calls.

The Smith Brothers . . . because Creighton guards Gary Swain and Renard Edwards coughed up the ball so much.

Anthony (Razor) Shines . . . because of the slicing line drives this outfielder hit in junior college. Not a bad nickname considering he could have just as easily ended up with Monkey. Razor's career came to a logical—and meteorological—end in Montreal, where the Expos briefly endured Tim Raines and Shines.

Brad (Q-Tip) Lohaus . . . because this Iowa center is very tall (7'), very thin (210) and has kinky blond hair. (Pitcher Jerry Reuss isn't so tall or thin, but he's called Q-Tip, too.)

Derrick (Band-Aid) Chievous . . . because this fluid forward, a notorious cut-up at Missouri, wears one someplace on his person whenever he takes to the court. Before retiring, he'll affix his current strip on the wall next to his bed. "I usually get six hours' sleep a night," said

Derrick (Band-Aid) Chievous

Chievous, a Queens native, while at Mizzou. "But I only get five out here, because of the time difference."

AND MEET MY BROTHER, STUDIO 54 M.

Were it not for his dad, Oakland R&B deejay Frankie M., Zenon M. might still be known as the relatively ordinary Zenon Middleton. Instead, Frankie Middleton tooled by the courthouse one day and had his surname legally changed to M., which had been his nickname. Son Zenon, who played a little hoop as a 6'7" forward at Cal Poly, Pomona, was quite content to carry on the family initial. "I'm not tired of it," quoth M. *fils,* who's also known as Z. "It's still fun. My girlfriend likes it and if anything it's been a help with girls. Everybody is curious."

Mmmm. Zzzzzzz.

Rollie (Waldo) Fingers . . . because "He looked like he should be a Waldo," according to former Brewers teammate Ted Simmons.

Carroll (Beano) Cook . . . because this avuncular college football commentator moved with his family from Boston to Pittsburgh as a kid, and was quickly dubbed the Boston Baked Bean by neighborhood playmates. They soon began calling him Beano, though to this day his mother never has. (It was Cook, in his role as sports information director at Pittsburgh in the 1950s, who tried in vain to persuade polio vaccine inventor Jonas Salk, then on the Pitt faculty, to pose for a publicity photo with a basketball player Cook was pushing for All-America honors. Cook wanted to bill the picture as "The World's Two Greatest Shotmakers.")

Bill (The Owl Without a Vowel) Mlkvy . . . because this All-America forward for the Temple Owls, though not possessing an A, E, I, O or U, *did* possess a pretty fair J. That jumper helped him set a since-broken NCAA single-game record of seventy-three points during the 1950–51 season.

Rollie (Waldo) Fingers

Stan (The Hurt) Williams . . . because "You shake hands with him," said a Yankee teammate, "and you'll be out for a week."

LOOKING FOR A FEW GOOD FANS

Sports fans, never known for being impartial, in recent years have become downright martial. Meet the paramilitants of the last two decades. They sit in the reserve seats:

Arnie's Army. These gallery foot-soldiers responded more to an Arnold Palmer one-putt than to cries of "Ten-hut!" before goose-stepping on to the next green.

Tway's Twoops. Twue fans of golfer Bob Tway, they surround tees and hang from twees to see their man, whether he's atop the leader board or twiple-bogeying.

McHale's Army. Boston Garden denizens who pledge their allegiance to Celtic forward Kevin McHale by flying a balcony banner. After the armed farces of TV's *McHale's Navy.*

The Marino Corps. Miami quarterback Dan's fans, whose dress code transforms the Orange Bowl into the Camouflage Bowl for Dolphin home games.

Rambis Youth. Dedicated not to fascism but to the fast break, these kids wear the same black combat glasses that their hero, Laker forward Kurt Rambis, wears—right down to the white tape on the nose bridge.

Gerela's Guerillas. Foot soldiers, as it were, loyal to Pittsburgh Steelers placekicker Roy Gerela. They'd lay in wait in the end zone.

(Arnie's Army)

THEY'RE ONLY HUMAN

 Mike (The Human Rain Delay) Hargrove . . . because of the seemingly endless series of gestures and motions he performs—between all pitches—before stepping into the batter's box.

 Jimmy (The Human) Rayl . . . because this Jim was so slim during his 1950s heyday at Indiana.

Marvin (The Human Eraser) Webster . . . because of his many days spent with Morgan State and the NBA's Sonics swatting opponents' shots into the men's room. By the end of his career with the Knicks, Webster was about as fierce a shot-blocker as TV's "Webster," 4' Emmanuel Lewis. And when Milwaukee picked him up, coach Don Nelson bought a Knick exec a Coke, describing it as compensation.

Dominique (The Human Highlight Film) Wilkins . . . because this one-man audio/visual show was an A/Viator extraordinaire even in high school, where he received his 'Niquename.

WHO SAYS IT'S DEHUMANIZING?

Boxing has given us Ed (The Human Freight Car) Dunkhorst, Harry (The Human Windmill) Greb, Joe (The Human Punching Bag) Grim, Harry (The Human Scissors) Harris and Henry (The Human Skyscraper) Johnson.

JUST FOR THE FUNK OF IT

"Zoid!" screams Atlanta Hawks coach Mike (Ditto) Fratello to his superstar forward, Dominique Wilkins, from the bench. "Run the two-

Jimmy (The Human) Rayl

down, Zoid!" Consider for a moment: Fratello was called Ditto as a New York Knicks assistant for his alleged similarities to then-boss Hubie Brown. Yet with all the other names Wilkins goes by—The Human Highlight Film, 'Nique and 'Nique-a-Zoid—why would Fratello choose Zoid, a truncation of the latter, which pays homage to the George Clinton–Parliament Funkadelic coinage "Freak-a-Zoid"? We have no way of knowing. But we *do* know that any coach who refers to one of his players as Zoid couldn't really be Hubie Brown's ditto.

Willie (The Say-Hey Kid) Mays . . . because "When I first came up to the Giants, I didn't know anybody's name. So I'd holler, 'Say hey, over there!' The sportswriters picked it up." And hung on to it, as if it were a drive off the bat of Vic Wertz.

Leroy (Supersub) Byrd . . . because this 5'6" Kentucky Wildcat was such a versatile reserve—though it's hard to imagine him at any position other than guard. Commentator Bucky Waters was so impressed with Byrd's versatility that he once said, "He can sit on your bench, or under it."

Alfred (Billy) Martin . . . because his face was one that only an Italian grandmother could love. It was Grandmamma who called the newborn Martin *bellissimo,* which was shortened to Billy, which, in turn, was lengthened to Banana Nose by kids in his tough West Berkeley neighborhood.

Jeff (Emergency) Ward . . . because this kicker won so many games for Texas during the mid-1980s with last-second field goals.

(Slavery) Avery Brundage . . . because this autocratic and controversial executive director of the International Olympic Committee, who commanded the Olympic movement for two decades that ended in the debacle of the 1972 Olympics in Munich, steadfastly refused to permit a relaxation of the Games' stringent amateur code.

And, no doubt, because it rhymes.

THEY PLAYED STRING MUSIC

At the outset of the 1957–58 season, Kentucky basketball coach Adolph (Baron) Rupp was heard to moan about the sorriest lot of holdovers he'd had to work with in a long time. "I got a collection of fiddlers when I need violinists," he said. "Oh, they're pretty good fiddlers; be right entertaining at a barn dance. Unfortunately, we're not scheduled to play any barn dances. To play in Carnegie Hall, you need concert violinists—and I ain't got any of those."

Later, he'd have a diminutive band of overachievers that became known as Rupp's Runts. But the Baron's *Fiddlin' Five* turkey-trotted their way through the 1958 NCAA tournament, defeating an Elgin Baylor-led Seattle team for the championship. It was Rupp's fourth NCAA title, and one that gave him disproportionate satisfaction. "My fiddlers?" said the Baron, referring to the obscure quintet of Vernon Hatton, Johnny Cox, Adrian Smith, Ed Beck and John Crigler. "They fool around and fool around with maybe two or three minutes to go. I'm not too happy—and then they get busy and win by one or two points."

FAMOUS NAMES

Charlie (Rembrandt) Leibrandt . . . because, as Kansas City teammate Willie Wilson said, "The man can paint." Corners, not canvases.

Floyd (Freud) Patterson . . . because he was brooding and introspective.

Vince (Vincent Van Go) Coleman . . . because Cardinal manager Whitey Herzog gave his speedster the perpetual green light. Coleman was originally called Mercury Swift by Lonnie (Skates) Smith, but that nickname has since been put on ice.

Wally (Charles Dickens) Backman . . . because this veteran Mets second baseman was with the team during the best of times and the worst of times.

THE THRILLA IN MANILA

It was a great title fight, an even greater fight title, and in the end *The Greatest* won a 14-round TKO of Smokin' Joe. Had the Thrilla in Manila been held somewhere else—say Bophuthatswana—it probably would have gone down simply as Ali-Frazier III. But promoter Don King doesn't do things by the numerals, Roman or otherwise. So for weeks before that 1975 fight in the Filipino capital, he and Muhammad Ali touted the bout as a thrilla. (It was a titular standard Ali would live up to on subsequent occasions, with the Rumble in the Jungle and the Drama in Bahama.) And in the standard pre-collision derision, Ali wore a T-shirt referring to Frazier as "The Manila Gorilla," predictably predicting that he'd smoke Joe. By the time Frazier's manager, Eddie Futch, threw in the towel just before the bell for the 15th round, Ali had proven he was no Manila folder. And the fight had lived up to its considerable billing.

HAIR'S TO THEM

 Diego (Pelusa) Maradona . . . because Argentina's greatest star has an abundant scalp full of it. (*Pelusa* is the Spanish word for hair.)

SMOOTH HANDLES

Nicknames were all that sprouted from the barren scalps of guards Donald (Slick) Watts and Fred (Curly) Neal, charter members of basketball's clean-bean club.

 Kyle (Vitalis) Macy . . . because that's the substance that this incorrigibly straight and neatly groomed guard is suspected of abusing, though only his hairdresser knows for sure.

 Dick (Dick Vitalis) Vitale . . . because he too never has a hair out of place, though in his case that's not such a big achievement. The basket-

Dick (Vitalis) Vitale

ball coach-turned-broadcaster is also known as "Coach," because that's what star players call Vitale in many apocryphal lunchtime conversations. "I was talking to Magic Johnson yesterday," Vitale is fond of saying, "and he says to me, 'Coach Vitale, what's the matter with my jumper?' "

COIFS TO QUAFF TO

Baseball players let no head of hair, or head of bare, go unnoticed. Nicknames, so often given off the top of the head, are sometimes inspired by the same spot.

Haircuts give rise to many. Chili Davis, the erstwhile Charles Theodore, was branded in high school when he was given a cut by a barber whose only apparent tools were a chili bowl and a razor. Earl Weaver's permanent gave rise to a temporary nickname in Baltimore, where Orioles saw his poodle 'do and dubbed their manager Fifi. Rick Cerone's curly, misshapen coif is why the catcher is called Spongehead.

The Mets' balding catcher is Gary (Almost) Carter to his teammates, so-called because he's almost Art Howe, the baldest player in the major leagues. Lack of hair, however, is not the problem with Tim Stoddard. The hirsute reliever is called Chewbacca, after the furry, bear-like creature in *Star Wars.* (At first glance, Stoddard doesn't appear to be too hairy. Says one baseball insider: "You have to see him naked to understand.")

And then there's Bill (Moose) Skowron, whose nickname is also hair-related, and not derived from his stature, as most think. No, Moose didn't use mousse. It seems, instead, that whenever Skowron's grandpa finished cutting his grandson's hair, young Billy looked like Benito Mussolini.

SAY WHAT?

When someone asks you "What's a Hoya?" the correct response is, "You're absolutely right." Time was when Georgetown students chanted *hoya saxa,* a Latin phrase meaning "What rocks," in support of their teams. The *saxa,* or rocks, was dropped, but the *hoya* remained as a nickname. And that's how Patrick Ewing became a Georgetown What.

Christy (Big Six) Mathewson . . . because the very fastest engine in the New York City Fire Department's stable at the turn of the century was called Big Six. Giants fans knew this because, when they weren't watching Matty douse rallies, they enjoyed following hooks-and-ladders to an entertaining local blaze. The Giants' Big Six was a member of the Big Five, the original quintet of Hall of Fame inductees, and earned Six Big strikeout titles with his legendary, incendiary fastball. No wonder, then, that when a fan scrawled only a large "6" on an envelope containing a letter to his idol, Mathewson received it.

Seattle (Huey) Slew . . . because Paula Turner, wife of trainer Billy Turner, called this colt Baby Huey for the way he waddled around the track the first time she saw him work out. Just as Seattle Slew wasn't half-bad, Baby Huey turned out to be wholly inappropriate.

Elbert (Golden Wheels) Dubenion . . . because this precious Buffalo Bills receiver was as fast as any chariot. Conservative congressman Jack Kemp, as Buffalo's quarterback, was on the supply side of most of Golden Wheels' receptions. By the way, remember Golden Richards? That was his real name.

(Poosh 'Em Up) Tony Lazzeri . . . because, while Italian fans at Yankee Stadium expected the *Bambino* to clear the bases with one swat, they asked of Lazzeri only that he advance the runners.

Jack (Murph the Surf) Murphy . . . because this multitalented gentleman, who played a violin solo with the Pittsburgh Symphony, stole the Star of India sapphire, was convicted of murder and found Christ during a life that included twenty-one years in prison, also won a raft of national surfing titles.

TEAM EFFORTS

The Osceola Astros . . . because this Houston Astros' Class A farm club in Osceola County didn't want to use the name of the Florida city in which they play. Otherwise they'd be the Kissimmee Astros.

The Pittsburgh Maulers . . . because Edward DeBartolo, chief of this USFL outfit, also owns several shopping malls.

The Houston Gamblers . . . because Kenny Rogers was part-owner of this USFL franchise and, as columnist Bernie Lincicome says, "It sure beats the Cowards or the Lucilles."

ALPHABET HOOP

Basketball is a game of X's and O's—and T's and Q's, and K's and V's, and an eyechart's worth of other letters that could fill up the *Wheel of Fortune*. These letters, you see, are the nicknames of players and coaches; if the game goes into OT, you'll want this bunch in there, ASAP:

Terry (T) Tyler. Guard. NBA fans from Detroit to Sacramento know that T-time has nothing to do with crumpets or golf clubs, but rather with someone who heats up in a hurry. For sheer brevity of handle, T beats out the Big O.

Quintin (Q) Dailey. Guard. With sexual assault charges and drug problems to his discredit, Q hasn't followed every letter of the law.

Xavier (X) McDaniel. Forward. X doesn't always mark the spot, but he usually spots his mark—and hits it.

Orlando (O) Woolridge. Forward. Why him? As the Sugarhill Gang opined in *Rapper's Delight:* "We need a man/Who's got finesse/And his whole name/Across his chest." That's Woolridge, who wears his nickname on his chest, in the form of the number 0.

Artis (The A-Train) Gilmore. Center. He brings some (alphabetical) order to the offense, and therefore gets the nod over The Big E, Elvin Hayes.

Oscar (The Big O) Robertson. Sixth man. We need a vowel in this spot, for you can hardly spell anything without one, and our sixth man will have to spell our other players off the bench.

Mike (Coach K) Krzyzewski. Assistant coach. As head coach at Duke, he led his team to the 1986 NCAA Championship game, which is why most folks know his name's pronounced Shuh-SHEF-skee. We think.

Jim (Coach V) Valvano. Assistant coach. Has also been called The Weasel, 'cause he looks like one.

Tom (The Alphabet Man) Abatemarco. Head coach. The fastidious head man at Lamar tends to every detail, from A to Z; it's a trait he picked up while minding his P's and Q's as an assistant coach to Coach V at North Carolina State. As head coach, he'll have to announce the cuts to Ernie D, World B, Dr. J and Special K.

(Tricky Dick) McGuire . . . because of this heady NBA guard's deceptive ball-handling abilities. Watergate buffs and casual basketball fans have, on occasion, erroneously assigned the nickname to Norm Nixon.

Stan (The Man) Musial . . . because he cut up the Dodgers in one phenomenal series in 1946 at Ebbets Field, and impressed Brooklynites dubbed him with his now-glorious Manhandle.

The Seven Blocks of Granite . . . because of the formidability of the Fordham offensive lines of 1936–37. Some of their real names—Al Babartsky, Alex Wojciechowicz, Vince Lombardi—are as tough as their nickname.

BAR GAME #1/ EXPUNSION FRANCHISES

Macon, Georgia was once home to the Whoopees. The Macon Whoopees, a minor league hockey team that would make Bob Eubanks proud, has inspired others to create fictitious new teams from cities and countries the world 'round. Expunsion franchises have opened in Alaska—the Juneau Whats and Nome Chomskys both play there—and in cities in the lower forty-eight. The Charlotte Tans, Norman Conquests, Greenwich Village Idiots, Augusta Wind, Montgomery Ward and Cleveland Amory are all domestic products.

Expunsion teams fare best, however, in cities abroad, where the sports market is still untapped. The Malta Milks and Brussels Sprouts have popped up (in the minds of expunsionists) in recent years, while the Algiers Hisses and Bergen Edgars have also burst upon the scene.

Radio/TV/newspaper man Larry King enjoys giving his new teams nicknames with an appropriate twist. He has written of the Atlanta Cablenets, Utah Tabernacles, Phoenix Seniors and Miami Cokes. It's more fun, however, to give birth to names that are appropriately *twisted.* Don't forget to flesh out your teams with some personality, no matter how sketchy.

The Nice Guys, for instance, will most certainly finish last. Then there are the Havana Good Times, whose season-ticket promotional brochure reads: "Havana Good Times—Wishin' You Were Here." The Dublin Cubes play backgammon, and the Muscat Love is the Middle East's first professional tennis team. The Greece Mypalms? Notorious point-shavers.

The nickname needn't be the least realistic. Some can, to be sure, such as the Crimea Rivers. Some cannot, as the Bolivia Newton-Johns indicate. (What's a Newton-John?) Then there are those that fall somewhere in between. The Port-au-Prince Spaghetti Knights conjure up an image of *something*, though it's difficult to say exactly what that something is.

Now you can't wait to get started naming your own expunsion franchises, can ya? Kenya? The Kenya Believeits, a surprising team of upstarts from Africa, won their sixth straight . . .

Mike (Scuffy) Scott . . . because Cubs manager Jim Frey accused this pitcher of scuffing baseballs on the mound. To the dismay of Houston poets, Scuffy joined the Astros the year after pitcher Mike (Buffy) LaCoss left.

Eamonn (Chairman of the Boards) Coghlan . . . because of this Irish record-holder's domination of the indoor mile. The nickname, in fact, is more of a title, passed from one king of the indoor mile to the next.

Walter (Sweetness) Payton . . . because this Sugar Bear's running certainly has "the quality of being sweet," which is the dictionary definition of Payton's nickname. He also must have the quality of being wheat. One wonders why a guy called Sweetness would hawk Wheaties, and not a more sugar-smacked cereal like Kaboom.

Al (Scoops) Oliver . . . because O, a first baseman, can't play D. If Scoops really could make a scoop, well, then you'd have one.

CALLED STRIKES

Catchers call for 'em, and umpires call 'em like they see 'em. Others have called pitches more creatively:

The Uncle Charlie is the simple curve ball, avuncular and good-natured. A good curve is properly executed, while a bad one always hangs. (Charlie's more straightforward cousin, the fastball, is merely Chucked.)

The Lord Charles is an Uncle Charlie with a pedigree: a breaking ball that winters at the Breakers; in short, a bender that ain't returned to sender.

Fernando's Fadeaway is Fernando Valenzuela's unhittable screwball—after the screwball musical comedy number "Hernando's Hideaway."

The Bo Derek was Tug McGraw's curve. Like the curvaceous actress with the corn-row coif, McGraw explained, the pitch had a "nice little tail on it." *The Peggy Lee* was McGraw's name for his underwhelming fastball, which left batters wondering, "Is That All There Is?" The Tugger tried to avoid uncorking his *Cutty Sark* ("it sails"), or his *Frank Sinatra* ("After they swing and connect, it's 'Fly Me to the Moon' ").

The Eephus Pitch was thrown rainbow fashion by Rip Sewell, who asked batters to Pardon My Blooper. It was named by teammate Maurice (The Belgian Bomber) Van Robays " 'cause it's a nothin' pitch, and eephus ain't nothin'."

The Dead Fish is Bob Ojeda's floundering change-up.

Cooled Heat is how they describe Floyd Youmans's stuff in Montreal. The phrase is an oxymoron, kind of like "Expos' consistency."

The Titanic is Dan Quisenberry's supposedly unsinkable pitch. "But when it starts to go down, it can be a real disaster."

The Ecological Fastball, Allen Ripley swears, never goes more than fifty-five miles an hour.

Rickey (Imperial) Gallon . . . because this former Louisville frontcourt star fueled Cardinal coach Denny Crum's early efforts there.

Walter (Sweetness) Payton

Jim (Bad News) Galloway . . . because he worked as a telegrapher while playing semipro ball, and in order to get away for games, had a colleague in another office wire him with the news that a relative had died—this before *every* game. Bad News played in twenty-one games with the Cardinals before being forced to travel fast.

Marvin (Bad News) Barnes . . . because of this forward's stern on-court demeanor and troubled off-court career, which included a stay in St. Louis with the ABA Spirits. ("Right nickname for that team," former Spirit Steve Jones has said. "Greatest collection of head cases in basketball history.") Barnes, who fondly referred to himself in the third-person familiar, once missed a Spirits' team flight. No prob: He chartered a jet, arrived after tip-off and still went for big numbers. Teammates saw Marvin stroll into the arena dressed in mink, with a Big Mac in each hand. "Have no fear," he said, *"News* is here."

Edouard (Newsy) Lalonde . . . because this hockey Hall of Famer, an original Montreal Canadien, had worked as a linotype operator during his youth.

Bill (Swish) Nicholson . . . because of his blustery swing, which always seemed to produce a strikeout or a bleacher shot.

SUGARS & ROCKYS

Even when only one boxer sported the nickname Sugar, the sweet science was too rich for Jake LaMotta. "I fought Sugar Ray so many times," raged the Bull, "it's a wonder I didn't get diabetes." He was talking of Ray Robinson, whom writer Jack Case once called "sweet as sugar," thus beginning a reign of cane that would see Sugar prefixed to countless boxing Raymonds. Many were saccharine pretenders: If Robinson was sweet as sugar, a palooka named Sugar Ramos was Sweet 'n' Low. And while Ray Leonard put some punch in Sugar again, the name still ranks second in the fight world.

In the ring, the first name in first names is Rocky. Rocky Marciano was Rocky to everyone, yet he was given a nickname (the Brockton

Blockbuster) that just hung around uselessly, like a member of Leon Spinks's entourage. Derived from Rocco, Rocky is indigenous to Italians, of course—Rocky Schmeling is as ridiculous as Sugar Graziano—and it's a name with tremendous appeal, as Sylvester Stallone has shown in a few films. Sly's opponents—Apollo Creed, Clubber Lang, Ivan Drago—are more decoratively dubbed, but it's Rocky Balboa (given fleeting mention as the Italian Stallion) whose name is best-loved on the large screen.

And on the small screen. Bullwinkle and Sugar doesn't quite cut it.

Robert (Rocky) Bleier . . . because, shortly after he was born, the child's proud papa declared, "The son of a bitch looks like a little rock." Now the Rock has a son of his own; the boy's nickname is Whiz, but his real name is Adri, which is Hebrew for *from the rock.*

Micheal (Sugar) Ray Richardson . . . because as a Knick and Net, he was so sweet. Unfortunately, Sugar's now better known for another white substance.

Bill (Sugar) Gullickson . . . because he's diabetic.

Lou Smith, sports editor of the *Cincinnati Enquirer,* quite sensibly trying to put a stop to a McCarthy-era movement to change the nickname of his city's baseball team from Reds to Red Stockings: "Let the Russians change. We had it first."

THE ROD SQUAD

No time capsule could capture the last three decades of American culture as the nicknames of three basketball players named Rodney have.

When Rod Hundley joined the Minneapolis Lakers in 1957, there was nothing cooler than drag racing—or just plain cruisin'—in a souped-up Chevy. Heaven forbid you should have to drive Dad's

DeSoto. And while Hundley wasn't a prolific scorer, he became known nonetheless as Hot Rod.

Hot Rod Hundley's career waned in the early 1960s as the Space Race escalated. At the end of the decade NASA was flourishing, man would walk on the moon and another Rod was being launched into basketball orbit. He was Rod Foster, who soon became known as Rocket Rod at UCLA.

Rod (Rocket Rod) Foster

Rocket Rod Foster graduated to the NBA as the country rolled further into the nuclear age. It would only be appropriate that the story end here, with the next great Rodney of Hoop being dubbed Fission Rod. Alas, it isn't to be. DePaul guard Rod Strickland, an electrifying playmaker, is introduced—by a hometown P.A. announcer with no sense of history—as Lightning Rod instead.

Phil (Flip) Saunders . . . because that's what you get when you say "Phillip" fast. Both a prize recruit and a prized recruiter at Minnesota, Saunders was wooed to the Tulsa staff by master motivator J. D. Barnett, who no doubt can't wait 'til his assistant takes ill, so he can implore his team to "Win one for the Flipper."

George (Sparky) Anderson . . . because "A sportswriter in Fort Worth in 1955 wrote about sparks flying because I argued with umpires. Then it was just Sparky. But I think of myself as George."

Much-Maligned (Chris) Bahr . . . because, in the words of this veteran kicker, "My wife thinks that's my first name. Every time she reads a story about me, that's always in front of my name."

The Wheeze Kids . . . because Pete Rose, Joe Morgan and Tony Perez comprised a Big Red Machine gone gray—and gone to Philadelphia. In the early 1980s, three decades after the Whiz Kids played, the Phillies had the oldest team in baseball.

PROFESSIONAL ATHLETES

Roger (The Woodchopper) Kingdom . . . because this Olympic gold medalist hurdler, who holds that the shortest distance between start and finish is a straight line, knocks over most of the hurdles in his path.

Sal (The Barber) Maglie . . . because his fastball could trim a batter's tresses and cause a little bloodletting at the same time. Maglie, who

Pete Rose (The Wheeze Kids)

once fired a depilatory missile at Richie Ashburn when Ashburn was on deck, had no qualms with being called the Barber. "It beats bein' called the Shoeshine Boy," he said.

Tom (The Exterminator) Henke ... because he routinely rids American League parks of opposing batters, rallies and other unwanted pests in his relief appearances.

George (The Iceman) Gervin . . . because this poker-faced guard exuded cool, and his physique—"PUR," his San Antonio Spurs jersey seemed to read, with each "S" disappearing under his armpits—suggested an icepick. Brother Derrick, a.k.a. the Icecube, remembers his brother walking on tiptoes back in Detroit: "A cool walk. A real cool walk." Gervin, again referring to that bod, calls himself the Bone, though he'll occasionally lapse into Ice. A former nemesis once apologized to Gervin for some past misunderstanding. Said Gervin: "Jesus Christ forgave. Why not Ice?"

George (The Iceman) Woolf . . . because this legendary jockey was known for how he "sat chilly" in the saddle—that is, stayed calm until the time came to make his move.

Bob (The Elevator Man) Staak . . . because, during this coach's playing days at Connecticut, teammates threw him the ball knowing full well that "it's going up."

Karl (The Mailman) Malone . . . because nothing can stay this NBA forward from the swift execution of his appointed 'bounds. In short, The Mailman always delivers.

Mark (The Fishin' Magician) Pavelich . . . because of his wizardry with a hockey stick and a fishing pole. He rejoiced in his trade from the New York Rangers and Manhattan's manholes to his native Minnesota and some right fine fishin' holes. Which begs the question some Iowans like to ask: How did the Minnesotan die while ice fishing? Why, he was run over by the Zamboni.

Waite (The Pitchin' Mortician) Hoyt . . . because this son of an undertaker was always willing to pitch in for Dad when not pitching for the Yanks. It's said he once picked up a body on his way to Yankee Stadium, leaving the corpse in the car while he threw a shutout.

ETTE-YMOLOGY

About the time we were given chairwomen and spokespeople, somebody—perhaps Mary Queen of Mascots—decreed that collegiate nicknames, too, needed to have their consciousnesses raised. Understandably, women athletes didn't like being called Bulldogs or Redmen, and their complaints engendered gender-conscious nicknames for distaff teams.

At many schools, adding a suffix to the men's nickname sufficed. Such *ette*-ymology produced Rattlerettes (Florida A&M), Bulldogettes

George (The Iceman) Gervin

Karl (The Mailman) Malone

(Tougaloo [Miss.] College) and Tigerettes (Mississippi Industrial College). Frette not over logic: female tigers are *not* called tigerettes . . . but we tigress.

Ladys first is the rule elsewhere. The search for contradistinction had brought some curious contradictions in many such cases. Providence Lady Friars? South Carolina Lady Gamecocks? Delta State should go with Statespeople, because their Lady Statesmen defeats the purpose. Lest you think *Lady* is just a prefix, Centenary College, where the men's teams are called Gentlemen, also fields Ladies, period.

In light of all this, we're happy to report that there are schools where the Lady's been a-trampled. Southern Cal's female version of the Trojans is the Women of Troy—a cumbersome, if classical, solution avoided by Taylor (Ind.) University. They're Tro*janes.* Its just plain Janes at the University of Puerto Rico, Mayaguez, where the men's teams are the Tarzans.

Gender *Jeopardy.* The answer is: The female counterpart to the Mountaineers at the College of the Ozarks. *Bzzzzzzzz!* What are the *Mountaindears*? Good question. Next: The ladies' teams at Louisiana State, where the men are known as Tigers. *Five seconds, please.* Who are the *Ben-Gals*?

Sammy Davis, Jr., must have had a bejeweled hand in nicknaming the women at the University of Georgia. For a long time they were Bulldog Babes. And we mean that, babe. Northern Arizona adopted the name Lumberjacks in 1909, and Lumberjills came tumbling after. At Angelo (Tex.) State, the men should take the lead from the women— the Rambelles. Wouldn't it be more macho for the males—who are the Rams—to become Rambeaus?

Okay. The men's teams at Salisbury State College in Maryland are the Sea Gulls. What are the women? Lady Gulls? Gullettes? Sea Gals, perhaps? Nope. They're She Gulls.

Eric (Rerun) Gregg . . . because this umpire weighed 357 pounds and resembled the heavy on TV's "What's Happening!" It was the Atlanta Braves who first called him Rerun, but the Philadelphia Phillies used the less subtle Fat Albert. In one run-in, Phillies manager Dallas Green used both. "He called me Rerun," Gregg recalls. "And then he threw in a Fat Albert 'Hey hey hey.' " Gregg had the last belly laugh, however, by shedding more than a hundred pounds—and at least two nicknames.

 Dave (The Glacier) Pezzuoli . . . because this lineman, a fixture at Pitt and in the NFL, is said to move no more than a few feet a year.

Albert (Dig 'Ems) King . . . because this NBA forward's skinny legs resemble those of Dig 'Ems the Frog, the spokesamphibian for Sugar Smacks cereal.

The Santo Clause . . . because this so-called "10/5" rule, which the Major League Baseball Players Association lobbied into existence to protect veterans with a certain amount of service from being involved in trades they opposed, was first invoked by the Cubs' Ron Santo. Ho, ho, ho; no, no, no.
hn,1;dn,26

SCREWBALLS

Remarking that the right half of the brain controls the left side of the body, and the left half of the brain controls the right side of the body, *Bill (Spaceman) Lee* once theorized that "Lefthanders are the only people in their right minds."

The Spaceman was a lefty, and that's where the theory collapses. The refreshing Lee pitched from so far out in left field that one Boston scribe was moved to write of The Ace from Space, another wag followed with Space Cowboy and a teammate, one John Kennedy, refined Lee's name to Spaceman.

(Dennis Eckersley, amazed by Lee's ability to paint the corners with his fastballs, called Lee *Sherwin Williams.* "His idea of a great painter," Lee said.)

When players arrive in the majors, they're expected to be fundamentally sound. *Mentally* sound is another question entirely. The mental makeup of baseball players has ranged from the outright Battey to the relatively Sain. The crazies, of course, are much more interesting:

Donnie (Lefty) Moore. "You've got to be crazy in this game," he says, "and everyone knows lefties are a little weird."

Tim (Loco) Ireland. This Oakland native aspires to the emperorship of Japan, and carries a negative ionizer on the road, to purge foreign hotel rooms of bad vibes.

Tim (Crazy Horse) Foli. When he takes to the road, he may still be sleeping at home. Or at second base, where he once bedded down after going 0-for-5.

Greg (Moon Man) Minton. "Nobody knows what he's thinking," says Joe Morgan. "He's in space somewhere." Perhaps in orbit with Lee. The reverent Moon will say only that "I don't do things the same way other people do."

Rich (Wacko) Dauer. Wacko is a description of his spikes-flyin', second-baseman-cryin', double-play-defyin' style of base-running.

Joaquin (Cuckoo Jar) Andujar. Just for laughs, call him Cuckoo Jar to his face. Ha! You see, he doesn't know that's what the rest of the league calls him!

Russ (The Mad Monk) Meyer. He was simply The Monk in high school, and he became Mad after one particular heated exchange with an umpire in Brooklyn. Before his disputin' earned him the Rasputin tag, Meyer was Russell the Redneck Reindeer.

Al (The Mad Hungarian) Hrabosky. This Fu Manchued pitcher was fond of stomping Hopi-like around the mound, pounding the ball into his glove and psyching himself up—and batters out—before each pitch.

Lou (The Mad Russian) Novikoff. Baseball's other Eastern bloc-head, whose first name/nickname/last name combination would fit pro wrestling like a tight one-piece.

Mark (Airhead) Littell. It's *nada* north of the eyebrows for Littell, baseball's biggest Daydream Reliever.

Don (Stan the Man Unusual) Stanhouse. One of the all-time greats, a Stan Musial of flakes. The only difference is that Stanhouse didn't play with the Cards—St. Louis *or* a full deck. Earl Weaver called him Full Pack, after the number of unfiltered Raleighs Stanhouse would aggravate him into smoking during strung-out relief appearances. It took twelve minutes to complete one memorable standoff with Mike (The Human Rain Delay) Hargrove, but Stanhouse had a reason for taking his time: "My stuff is so bad, the longer I hold on to the ball, the better my chances."

Frank (Toys in the Attic) Bertania. Given to him by Moe Drabowsky (who once dialed Hong Kong from the Anaheim bullpen and ordered a Chinese dinner to go) when both were pitching for Baltimore.

PATERS FAMILIAR

Eugene (Big Daddy) Lipscomb . . . because this NFL behemoth, who never went to college and died of an apparent heroin overdose, stood 6′6″ and weighed 290.

Phil (Father Time) Niekro . . . because Knucksie, as this knuckleballer is also known, is the oldest player in the majors. "How can the detectives tell Father Time he has to go to bed?" one Yankee asked when owner George (Boss) Steinbrenner began enforcing curfews. "He's older than they are."

James (Cool Papa) Bell . . . because, as this Negro Leagues star tells it, "the players said I looked cool out there, so they called me Cool. The manager said that wasn't enough and added Papa. That's how I became Cool Papa."

Tommy (The Godfather) Lasorda . . . because the Los Angeles Dodgers' Steve Sax once found in his bed the head of a pig with an apple in its mouth and a note that read: "Play better baseball—or else." It was signed "The Godfather." Not coincidentally, the special at Lasorda's restaurant that day was roast pork.

THE AMAZIN' A-LIASES

As owner of the Oakland A's (née Athletics), Charles O. Finley outfitted his outfit in gold-and-green polyester double-knit uniforms, complete with white spikes. It was the first time such tailoring and tincture had appeared on a major league diamond, much less appeared together.

James (Cool Papa) Bell

Finley himself favored multi-hued sportscoats and orange baseballs for use in night games.

It was no surprise, then, that Finley began calling pitcher John Odom "Blue Moon." The owner was always looking to make his team more colorful. "Charlie just wanted a colorful name," says Rene Lachemann, who was playing in the A's organization then. "No real reason." What *is* surprising is that Finley thought Vida *Blue*'s name also lacked sufficient color. In 1971, he asked Blue to legally change his first name to True. The pitcher balked. "Vida was my father's name," he said, being true, after all. "And every time I pitch I honor him."

Indeed, Finley signed a player in 1975 who would play five games and bat .000 for the A's. His value? A name that would never need nicking: Charlie Chant. The A's mascot, an enormous mule, was Charlie O. Charlie O—as in Owner—pulled off his biggest coup when he called Jim Hunter one off-season to talk contract. Hunter couldn't be reached at his North Carolina home. Seems he was out fishing for you-know-what, and he's been Catfish Hunter ever since. Only upon Hunter's election to the Hall of Fame did it come out that that was one big fish story, designed for the media's consumption.

It all makes one wonder what Finley, who's now retired, would have done to get his hands on the California Angels' reliever who has unwittingly nicknamed himself. He's Chuck (Don't Call Me Charlie) Finley.

M. L. Carr, then of the Detroit Pistons, at the height of the Muslim name-changing vogue in the NBA: "I think I'm going to change my name to Abdul Automobile."

THERE'S ONLY ONE

Paul (Bear) Bryant . . . because this coach once wrestled a bear at a carnival. (Would Alabama football have been the same if he had wrestled an alligator?)

Bryant (Tex) Pool . . . because, as his boss at Alabama, Paul (Bear) Bryant, explained to Pool, a former Crimson Tide assistant, "There's only one Bryant at Alabama."

Paul (Bear) Bryant

FAMOUS FRONTS

"Defense is an emotional game," veteran NFL defensive coordinator Bud Carson has said. "Its very nature lends itself to nicknames. And the greatest defenses were emotional defenses." That's why, in pro football, nearly every great D has had an a.k.a. In the 1970s, the Rams' front line was called the Fearsome Foursome. The original quartet featured Lamar Lundy, Merlin Olsen, Rosie Grier and Deacon Jones. But by Super Bowl XIV in 1980, the Rams' line was reduced to Fred Dryer and Jack Youngblood—a Gruesome Twosome that proved less than awesome against Pittsburgh's Steel Curtain of (Mean) Joe Greene, Ernie (Fat) Holmes, Dwight White and L. C. (Daddy Bags) Greenwood. Though the names have changed in Pittsburgh, the nickname for the defense hasn't. Fans in L.A., however, no longer root for the Fearsome Foursome, or even root for its square root.

Other superlative sack-seekers, with sobriquets:

(The Doomsday Defense)

(The Killer B's)

The Doomsday Defense. Pittsburgh twice survived Doomsday in Super Bowls X and XIII, and it has since been Armageddon for this alias of the Dallas Cowboys.

The Purple People-Eaters. The Minnesota Vikings' front four went oh-fer in four Super Bowls, and eventually died. "Anorexia," said the medical examiner.

The No-Name Defense. Comprised of Miami Dolphins defenders who made a collective name for themselves in Super Bowls VII and VIII.

The Killer B's. Rather than bearing no names, these fish of more recent spawning—Brudzinski, Baumhower, Betters, Bokamper, Bowser and the brothers Blackwood—gave alliteration a good name. B's sacks were, of course, called B's Whacks. Alas, "B's WAXED" read the headlines after Super Bowls XVII and XIX.

The New York Sack Exchange. The Jets bypassed Sacks Fifth Avenue in shopping for a nickname; they also eschewed Sacks and Violence. Despite the raised Dow Jones index fingers of considerable commodity Mark Gastineau, this front four of the early 1980s never reached a Super Bowl. Too NYSE, no doubt.

The Orange Crush. The name was first used by the Cleveland *Browns* in 1976, when they donned their pumpkin-colored pants, but it didn't really go down easy until Denver adopted it. That Bronc defense, out-D'ed indeed by the Doomsday in Super Bowl XII, is no longer named for the soft drink, even though its pop, once gone, has returned.

The Buc Stoppers. The Tampa Bay Bucs' D was passed as far as the desktop of the 1980 NFC championship game. The Buccaneers have been spent for a new nickname ever since.

The Silent Force. Washington Redskins linemen who made some noise in 1984. "We just do our job quietly," explained leader Tony (Mac the Sack) McGee, before being muzzled in the playoffs.

The Junkyard Dogs. The Chicago Bears considered their Super defense of 1985–86 to be composed of sundry Bad, Bad Leroy Browns. (Leroy, you'll recall, was described by troubadour Jim Croce as being both from the South Side of Chicago and "meaner than a junkyard dog.") But as the Browns' Dixon would observe, "Bears don't bark. They growl."

The Dawgs. In 1984, members of the Cleveland Browns' secondary began pumping up their linemen by telling them that coverage would be better if they went after the quarterback like hungry dogs. "We started barking at them to psych them up," explained defensive back Hanford (Top Dawg) Dixon. "Soon we were barking at each other." At first, as a Columbus *Citizen-Journal* headline proclaimed, they were ALL BARK, NO BITE. But by the end of 1985, the canine corps had taken the Brown's to the wire in the AFC semis before rolling over. Then, the following season, individual Dawgs were tagged—Bob (Mad Dawg) Golic and Carl (Big Daddy Dawg) Hairston—along with the Dawg Pound, the end zone section from which Cleveland fans threw so many dog biscuits during the AFC Championship Game that Broncos receiver Vance Johnson said he could feel them crunching underfoot. Alas, Denver won, and the Dawgs still hadn't had their day.

MONSTERS, MYTHS AND MUTANTS

Dave (Kong) Kingman . . . because he had the physical power of King Kong, but less respect for women: He once sent a live, gift-wrapped mouse to a female sportswriter he particularly disliked.

Dan (Danimal) Hampton . . . because he's supposed to be half Dan and half Animal, though this Bear's behavior on and off the field suggests a ratio other than 50–50.

Sean (Catman) Farrell . . . because New York Giants Jim Burt and Casey Merrill told teammate Joe McLaughlin that Farrell, a Tampa Bay offensive lineman, was afraid of cats. Farrell, not really a fraidy-cat, found McLaughlin, who lined up opposite him, meowing, clawing and purring "Caaatmaan." What did the Catman do? "After the game," a delighted Burt reported later, "Farrell comes up to me and says, 'What the hell's wrong with number 52? He thinks he's a cat.' "

Ed (The Troll) Ott . . . because, as a 5'10" catcher, he was intrepid in blocking the plate against larger baserunners. "I'm like that little troll under the bridge in fairy tales," Ott explains. "If you're going to cross my bridge, you're going to have to pay for it."

⚾ **Dick (The Monster) Radatz** . . . because this relief pitcher, who developed his frightening reputation with the Red Sox, stood 6′6″, weighed 230 pounds and could almost stare down the Green Monster.

⚾ **Mickey (Gozzlehead) Rivers** . . . because that's what John Milton (Mickey) Rivers calls everyone else, and what you say is what you are. "A gozzlehead is just, you know, like a bullfrog face," says Rivers.

Mickey (Gozzlehead) Rivers

Mailboxhead and Warplehead are also in his vocabulary. "A Warple-head, that's a different shape," says the Mick. "A funny-looking creature. Odd-shaped. Funny-looking."

Bob (The Geek) St. Clair . . . because of this NFL veteran's hearty appetite for exotic foods, including raw meat. When hunting them was legal, St. Clair once bagged fifteen doves and cut their hearts out.

"You gonna make some sorta sauce outta that?" asked his companion, a rookie from Nebraska.

"*Sauce?*" said the Geek. He then popped down the hearts like so many bonbons.

Randy (Manster) White . . . because this Cowboy is, as one teammate says, "half man, half monster."

THE SUPERSHILL

When broadcasting mogul Ted Turner bought the Atlanta Braves in 1976, he decided that his players should wear nicknames on their uniforms, a move that would make it difficult to tell the players even *with* a program. Roger Moret, for instance, wore *Gallo,* which is the Spanish word for "skinny." Not even Jerry Royster knew why he had Jaybird on his back. The most mysterious nickname, though, belonged to Andy Messersmith, whom Turner took to calling Channel.

We'll never know for certain whether this owed itself to Messersmith's presumed ability to throw accurately, or even to throw a ball from England to France. We *do* know that Captain Outrageous had the sobriquet sewn to the back of Messersmith's jersey, in place of his surname, and directly above his number 17.

The commissioner's office immediately stepped in, and Turner resumed calling his player "Andy" again. Who knows why the Commish put the kibosh on the owner? We'll assume it's sheer coincidence that WTBS, Turner's Atlanta-based SuperStation, is Channel 17 on your dial.

Elroy (Crazy Legs) Hirsch . . . because this former star at Wisconsin and with the Los Angeles Rams had a cartoon character's running style.

Garry (Jump Steady) Templeton . . . because young Garry took "at the hop" literally, jumping to rock music instead of dancing.

America's Team . . . because that was the title of the Dallas Cowboys' preseason highlight film in 1979. People were poking fun at the slow Pokes the next season, so in 1980 they changed the name of their highlight reel from *Team of the Decade* to the less pretentious *A Cut Above.* That didn't stop cynics from calling them, after a spate of reported drug problems, South America's Team.

Mike (Mitch the Stitch) Mitchell . . . because, unlike the many Taylors who have passed through the NBA, he makes his own clothes.

THEY NEVER MET, OR
INTERCONFERENCE MARRIAGES NEVER WORK
ANYWAY

The woman claimed to have never even *heard* of professional football; she certainly hadn't seen a game. Granted, this was 1966, when Thursday night editions of *Monday Night Football* were a mere gleam in television's probing eye. And, after all, the woman was a Cuban immigrant just arrived in America. But by the time she became a United States citizen in 1973, Maria de Los Angeles Rams had become a devotee of the game. So what if her favorite team was the Colts.

The same year Ms. Rams arrived in the States, the American Football League's new franchise in Miami held a contest, seeking a nickname for the team. One Robert Dolphin of Miami mailed in his entry with understandable aplomb. Dolphin's suggestion? The Miami Barracudas.

(Slingin') Sammy Baugh . . . because of his passing proficiency; this good ol' Baugh set the record for most touchdown tosses in a game with eight.

Jim (The Ivory Tower) Petersen . . . because this 6'10" forward comes off the Houston Rocket bench to spell Twin Towers Akeem Olajuwon and Ralph Sampson. Pigmentation problems prevent the *tour d'ivoire* from making the Twin Towers a set of triplets.

Fred (Dixie) Walker . . . because, though he made a name for himself in Brooklyn, he was born in the Land of Cotton. That fact became distressingly evident when the People's Cherce asked to be traded because the Dodgers had signed Jackie (Quicker'n You Can Say) Robinson.

Rod (Shrine Game) Hill . . . because he ran East and West but rarely forward while returning punts for the Dallas Cowboys.

TV A.K.A.'S

"The MacNeil/Lehrer Report": "You've often been called Johnny Hustle. Are you proud of that?"
   Pete Rose: "Johnny Hustle?"

So Robin and Jim don't watch a lot of baseball. Baseball players don't watch a lot of "MacNeil/Lehrer," or anything else on PBS, if nicknames are your Nielsens:
   Mark (Opie) Thurmond. Has the innocuous look of Opie Taylor from "The Andy Griffith Show"—until his fastball makes an Aunt Bea-line for your head.
   Mario (Isaac) Ramirez. From 'fro to Fu, he looks like Isaac, "The Love Boat's" bartender.
   John (Guido) Franco. He does a nifty impression of Father Guido Sarducci, the deposed Vatican City correspondent for "Saturday Night Live."

Claude (Gomer) Osteen. Gawww-awww-leeee does he look and sound like Jim Nabors, Camp Henderson's "Gomer Pyle."

Jim (Klinger) Gantner. Because he tripped over a base once, à la Corporal Max Klinger, who's always stumbling in his pumps on "M*A*S*H."

Darrel (Nort) Chaney. He wore "Nort" on his Braves uniform in 1976. Nort's short for Norton—"The Honeymooners'" Ed Norton.

Brian (Hulk) Downing. He was skinnier than Don Knotts before weightlifting gave him some incredible bulk. Now he looks more like Lou Ferrigno, late of "The Incredible Hulk."

Dwayne (Hazel) Murphy. For a 6'1" black guy, he really does look like Hazel Burke, the cherubic Irish maid on "Hazel."

The 1973 Twins' reserves called themselves *The F-Troop,* after the irrepressible castaway cavalry men on the old TV show. In 1985, the Mets did the same thing, appointing bench leader Rusty Staub as Sergeant O'Rourke and Clint Hurdle as Corporal Agarn, both "F-Troop" regulars.

DANCING CARDS

The California Quake . . . because Cowboys receiver Butch Johnson's end-zone boogie, though bred in Dallas, was birthed in the Golden State. This Quaker had to stop feeling his oats, however, when the league found fault with "excessive demonstration" afield.

The Boris Boogie . . . because Boris Becker follows winning strokes with a celebratory shuffling of his feet. This Teutonic two-step has become his trademark.

AVIATION APPELLATIONS

Tony (TWA) Wilson . . . because, from humble beginnings at Lexington's Douglass Park Skydome (" 'cause the only roof is the sky"), to stardom at Western Kentucky, Tony Wilson Airlines flew frequently.

Brian (Hulk) Downing

Air Coryell . . . because the San Diego Chargers, under coach Don Coryell, believed that the forward pass was the best way to light up the scoreboard.

Aer Lingus . . . because the pass-happy Holy Cross team of 1983 took off with many players of Irish descent.

AND IF YOU'RE AFRAID OF FLYING . . .

Ground Chuck . . . because the Seattle Seahawks, under coach Chuck Knox, preferred to run the ball on offense.

YAZ INDEED

His birth certificate requires twenty-two letters to identify Carl Michael Yastrzemski. Yankee fans could do it with four letters, but it only took three for Early Wynn.

Yaz.

One of baseball's most famous abbreviations owes itself to a most obscure alleviation—of Wynn's regular duties as a pitcher for the White Sox in 1961. He was playing out the last seasons of a twenty-four-year career, and Yastrzemski was a Red Sox rookie. Chicago announcer Bob Elson missed a plane one day and was unable to announce a game in Boston. Wynn, who wasn't scheduled to pitch, was summoned to fill in for Elson, and manager Al Lopez let him go for the afternoon.

"Well, that might have been the worst day of my life," says Wynn. "Here I'm a complete novice behind the mike, and I'm confronted with a guy named Yastrzemski." Yah-STREM-skee isn't impossible to pronounce, but it sure *looked* intimidating to Wynn. "It looked like alphabet soup," he says. "I tried pronouncing it a couple of times, but it was a nightmare."

But history was being made.

"Finally I said, 'Yaz is at bat,' " says Wynn. "And he's been Yaz ever since."

STOUTHEARTED MEN

Charles (The Round Mound of Rebound) Barkley . . . because, rounded to the nearest pound, the Mound carried no fewer than 275 at Auburn. In the pros the 6'6" Sixer would trim down; among the many things from his college days that no longer fit him were A-mana, Food World, Breadtruck, The Wide Load from Leeds and Boy Gorge.

Mickey (The Man Who Ate Manhattan Beach) Klutts . . . because he hails from that town on the California coast, a municipality that perfectly suited Klutts's see-food diet. Despite its subject's heft, this nickname is only a tertiary way of referring to Gene Ellis (Mickey [The Man Who Ate Manhattan Beach]) Klutts.

Lafayette (Fat) Lever . . . because of a corruption of his first nickname, "Fayette." After Fayette became Fat at Arizona State and Lever declared his eligibility for the NBA draft, rumors were rife that Golden State would select him. At an MVP luncheon, one sportswriter sauntered over to Al Attles's table, hoping to get a scoop from the Warriors general manager. "You gonna get Fat?" the wag asked. Replied Attles, who had just sat down to his meal, "I don't plan on eating *that* much."

Paul (MacFat) MacLean . . . because "When he first came to camp, we had to put him on a diet," says Winnipeg Jets general manager John Ferguson. "He was so fat you couldn't see his cheeks."

Carlton (Pudge) Fisk . . . because he was 5'4" and weighed 155 pounds in the eighth grade. "My grandmother or aunt must have hung it on me," Fisk laments. "I grew eight inches in one year, but that name stuck."

Charles Barkley (The Round Mound of Rebound)

IGNOMINIOUS COGNOMENS

These guys weren't Saints. Saints are flawless and infallible; this team was winless and laughable. Seeking anonymity, football fans bagged their heads and the team's official nickname during leaner seasons in New Orleans. Even now, when the Saints ain't winning, they're the Ain'ts. When any team is losing or scandal-rocked, the coach is the first to go. But the nickname is often second.

No strangers to the loss column but *playing* stranger with each game, the Texas Rangers didn't ring as true as the Texas Strangers did. After the football and hockey teams in Minnesota became comfortably ensconced in mediocrity, the Viqueens and No Stars found it difficult to shake their new handles. Bulls fans in Chicago took it out on the cheerleaders, denouncing the Luvabulls as the Horribulls. In Indianapolis, Colts quickly came to be known as an acronym for Count On Losing This Sunday.

And those paragons of tact, the Brotherly Lovers in the city thereof, didn't miss a beat when it was revealed that amphetamine use was rampant in their baseball team's clubhouse. Like the Ain'ts, Strangers and 'Queens, the Philadelphia Pillies had to live with their new name.

NASCAR publicist Chip Williams, on his racy nickname: "Women call me Dristan. I thought it was because I'm so long-lasting, but I found out it's because I make their noses run."

WILD KINGDOM

> *These are the saddest of possible words:*
> *"Tinker to Evers to Chance."*
> *Trio of bear Cubs and fleeter than birds,*
> *"Tinker to Evers to Chance . . ."*

If Franklin P. Adams thought the Cubs' Tinker-to-Evers-to-Chance double play combination (that's Joe-to-Johnny-to-Frank, 6-4-3 if you're scoring at home) full of animal imagery, he'd have delighted years later in the team's entire infield, which could inspire all sorts of zoological verse.

On this particular day, Steve (Rainbow) Trout is the starting pitcher. At first and second for the Cubs are a Bull and a Ryno, Leon Durham and Ryne Sandberg. The serpentine Larry Bowa *did* play shortstop, until rookie Shawon (Thunderpup) Dunston took his place. This left only the short-of-leg third baseman, Ron (The Penguin) Cey, and catcher Jody Davis to walk upright.

The only animal in the outfield is Keith (The Antelope) Moreland. Team leader Gary Matthews is Sarge, and he salutes the Bleacher Bums in his native left field each time he takes up his post there. In center, Bob Dernier goes by his given name, which is why Moreland is The Antelope. You see, everyone at Wrigley knows that the outfield is where Dernier and The Antelope play.

Gaylord (The Ancient Mariner) Perry . . . because of this pitching great's advanced years when he threw for Seattle. Ten years earlier he was being called Old Goat, but K-Y Jelly—the *slime* of the Ancient Mariner—kept this self-confessed spitballer around longer than most expected.

The Diaper Squad . . . because every member of the 1960 Orioles' pitching rotation—Chuck Estrada, Jack Fisher, Milt Pappas, Jerry Walker and Steve Barber—was twenty-two years old or younger.

Mike (Shaky) Walton . . . because he was always skating on thin ice—or skating off it—as a St. Paul Saint. In the waning minutes of one particularly bitter World Hockey Association playoff loss, Shaky motioned to his wife in the stands, requesting that she pull the car to the back of the arena. She did, and when the game ended, Shaky skated off the ice, walked down the tunnel and hopped, still in full uniform, into the getaway car.

(Sudden) Sam McDowell . . . because he gained quick fame with his quick fastball.

DOCTORS

It's the nickname world's oldest profession, that of Doctor, and certainly its most prestigious. Preachers and Deacons require divine assistance; even as some basketball Judges rule the court, others may sit on the bench. But Doctors are *always* revered—for their years of experience, their infinite wisdom or their superior ability to operate.

They first began practicing in baseball, which has employed more than sixty Docs since 1871. The title was usually conferred on sage veterans and, of course, those few players who had medical training.

To be sure, there are still a few M.D.s around nowadays. Physician George (Doc) Medich dispensed medical aid when he wasn't pitching; erstwhile Edmonton Oiler Randy (Doc) Gregg, M.D., has taken both a hipcheck and the Hippocratic oath. But medical examiners like Robert (Dr. Doom) Brazile and Steve (Dr. Death) Williams exist, as does Missouri basketballer Lynn (Doc Nice) Hardy. There are even Ph.D.s: Batting instructor Charlie Lau was baseball's foremost hitting theorist, and his most successful pupils—among them George Brett—bestowed upon him the inevitable degree: The Mysterious Dr. Lau. And there's Ferdie Pacheco, a curious combination of television boxing analyst and corner medicine man known to viewers as The Fight Doctor.

But most prominent are the surgeons of sports, Doctors renowned as smooth operators. For them, to *operate* means more than the dictionary's definition of "to work effectively." They get the job done with grace and precision and style. They're cool. These are the elite Doctors of Letters, Julius (Dr. J) Erving and Dwight (Dr. K) Gooden, at different times masters of their games. Doctors J and K stand alone in this branch of nickname medicine; in fact, in 1983, before Gooden was licensed, Temple University conferred a Doctor of Arts degree on Erving and said of The Good Doctor: "Now the word 'doctor' designates a poetic summit of sport reached only by him."

Julius (Dr. J) Erving . . . because he called a high school buddy named Leon Saunders "The Professor," and The Prof countered with "The Doctor" for the young J. The name passed muster at a summertime Rucker League game in Harlem, where the P.A. announcer tried "The Claw," "Black Moses" and a score of others before Erving walked over

Julius (The Doctor) Erving

and said "Just call me The Doctor." Roland (Fatty) Taylor gets credit for adding the J when Doc joined the ABA. Also a Jewel in his pre-med days.

Dwight (Dr. K) Gooden . . . because Dan Gooden used to drag to his young son's games an unsuspecting neighbor, who in turn would yell, "Come on, doctor, operate on him." Gooden took his place next to Julius Erving in the doctoral alphabet when he began striking out a storm in the majors, and Doctor, Doc and Dr. D gave way to Dr. K. He is sometimes called Doctor OK after merely ordinary outings; DOCTOR KO'ED, read the tabloids, after his hospitalization for cocaine addiction.

Felix (Doc) Blanchard, Jr., . . . because his father was a doctor. When Felix Sr. died and Blanchard went off to West Point, he became just Doc, and later Mr. Inside, the up-the-middle half of Army's "Mr. Inside and Mr. Outside" backfield of the mid-1940s.

Robert (Dr. Doom) Brazile . . . because he was the only linebacker at the 1975 College All-Star Game without a nickname. "We had Spiderman and Batman," recalled Brazile. "They took my name right out of the comics, right out of the Chicago *Tribune*." When Cardinal rookie Johnny Barefield tried to pass himself off as Dr. Doom in 1978, Brazile got uppity: "I don't know who he is, but my mother only gave birth to one Dr. Doom," he said. "And that's me."

Darrell (Doctor Dunkenstein) Griffith . . . because this guard created many a monster dunk while leading Louisville to the 1980 NCAA title. The chief resident of the Cards' Doctors of Dunk, his teammates just called him Stein—as in Dunkenstein, as in "In your mug," as in the second player chosen in the NBA "draught." (Less hip university types dubbed him Louisville's Living Legend.)

Abraham (Dr. Du) Okorodudu . . . because this Ivy League record holder (most syllables, full name; most vowels, last name) needed a community-college handle. Though his Penn pals called him the Good Doctor, Abe was a Dr. Du-little on the basketball court.

Felix (Doc) Blanchard

Darrell (Dr. Dunkenstein) Griffith

 Glenn (Doc) Rivers . . . because the shirt he favored at a Marquette basketball camp bore the likeness of Julius Erving. Marquette assistant Rick Majerus named him in eighth grade, but the demure Rivers demurs at comparisons to The Doctor. "There's really *no* comparison," he says. "I'm a guard and he's a forward." But with practice, Rivers believes, he might take up his own practice. "I'm not as good as Erving," he admits. *"Yet."*

Pat (Evil Doctor Blackheart) Smith . . . because fellow Warrior George Thompson recognized Smith's lazy eye and combative spirit at Marquette, and stuck him with the name as if Smith were a voodoo doll. Years later, deciding that Evil Doctor Blackheart was no longer apropos, Thompson came up with some new *Omen-*clature at an alumni game. "While it was a great name, I just decided he needed an update," he says. "So we decided to call him Damien."

Dick (Dr. Strangeglove) Stuart . . . because, though this bumbling first baseman was more akin to Inspector Clouseau, the bulk of his E-3s came in the early 1960s, when Peter Sellers was starring in *Dr. Strangelove*. A.k.a. *The Boston Strangler* and *Stonefingers*.

AND FOR *SERIOUS* PROBLEMS . . .

Mark (The Surgeon) Turgeon . . . because this tiny (5'9") Kansas guard, whose grandma had to take in the smallest jersey the Jayhawks could find for him, cut through defenses with the precision of a scalpel.

WHITE BREAD'S GOT NO RISE

In basketball especially, white-bread players don't inspire nicknames the way the flashier Wonders do. Witness Larry Bird. His name begs for an avian appellation, but his *game* prevents one—and he remains one of sport's superstars *sans* popular sobriquet. In other words, Tom Heinsohn remained Tom Heinsohn while being fundamentally sound; Connie Hawkins was The Hawk because his style was more Motown sound.

Dennis Johnson knew all about this phenomenon. When Charles Barkley looked more Caucasoid than Freak-a-Zoid in missing two tomahawk dunks against the Celtics, D. J. said of the Round Mound of Rebound, "He had plenty of Tom, but not enough Hawk."

MISTER-IES SOLVED

 Ernie (Mr. Cub) Banks . . . because of his nineteen years of service on Chicago's North Side. Wrigley-goers recognized that this Cub-for-life deserved a title that would do the importance of being Ernest one better.

Rickey (Mr. October) Brown . . . because this former Atlanta Hawks benchwarmer always seemed to have a training camp just spectacular enough to make the roster before disappearing for the regular season. Not to be confused with a certain erstwhile A, Oriole, Yankee and Angel, name of Reggie (Mr. October) Jackson, who had a fair World Series or two.

Glenn (Mr. Outside) Davis . . . because he was the end-around running mate of Doc (Mr. Inside) Blanchard (see p. 78). *Another* Glenn Davis plays first base for the Astros, but only Chris Berman (see p. 3) calls *him* Mr. Outside.

Eric (Mr. Benny) Dickerson . . . because—Oh, Rochester—he's cheap.

Paul (Mr. Potatohead) Guay . . . because this L. A. King's face appears to have been assembled by a three-year-old attaching appendages to the tuber-headed toy.

Kelvin (Mrs. Butterworth) Ransey . . . because then-teammate Mychal Thompson believed a four-year contract had made this squat Portland guard "thick and rich, like the syrup."

Larry (Mr. Goodwrench) Rembert . . . because, as a college freshman, he once suffered second-degree burns on his arms and chest while unscrewing the radiator cap on his car. The folks at the U. of Alabama, Birmingham gave their prize recruit condolences, a good ribbing and a nickname to go with the scars.

Glenn (Mr. Outside) Davis, Felix (Mr. Inside) Blanchard

Dave (Mr. Monday) Sann . . . because he played like Nicklaus in Monday tournament qualifying rounds, but would wind up nickel-less after faring poorly at week's end. He set a course record in one Monday qualifier, but made the cut after thirty-six holes in only three tourneys in two years, earning $1,828. Monday, Monday; can't trust that day.

Brook (Mr. Ed) Steppe . . . because this NBA journeyman had the look of a horse, of course, of course.

Marvin (Mr. Fuzzy) Stinson . . . because "my mother called me Fuzzy, 'cause that's the way my hair's always been. The kids added Mister out of respect."

Geoff (Mr. April) Zahn . . . because of this pitcher's extraordinary lifetime record during that supposedly cruel month.

NAMES WILL NEVER HURT ME

"Mr. Snipes" is written in script on the back of their shirts. Are they players on a softball team sponsored by a local hair salon?

No, they're the entourage that tends to boxer Renaldo (Mister) Snipes. "Mister" may not quite cut it. But ring names, those sensational aliases worn on robes and trunks, are meant to intimidate the guy in the other corner, who has an equally nasty handle on his trunks.

And boxers take 'em seriously.

Charles Hecker had a 5–9 record as Hecker the Wrecker, so after much soul-searching he decided to become Golden Boy. Unfortunately nobody told the Madison Square Garden ring announcer, who thought Hecker was still the Wrecker, and introduced him as such in the fighter's next bout. Hecker went berserk until a correction was finally announced, and had very little fury left. Golden Boy was knocked down and out in the second round, but when he *did* stand, it was on principle.

Ring names evolved as a means for promoters and newsmen to gussy up the low life who often become boxers. The monikers sometimes identify the fighter's hometown, and frequently come off sounding like the title of a Hemingway novel. George Godfrey was The Black

Shadow of Leiperville; Luis Firpo was The Wild Bull of The Pampas; and Max Schmeling was The Black Uhlan of The Rhine.

Now, no civilized pugilist would leave the gym without a truly barbaric ring name. Frank (The Animal) Fletcher sounds as polite today as (Gentleman) Jim Corbett did in the nineteenth century. Dennis (The Fist) Fykes, Hector (Macho) Camacho, Johnny (Bump City) Bumphus—mild monikers all. A bout between James (Bonecrusher) Smith and Kevin (Shock Treatment) Dickerson sounds like a minuet nowadays.

Harry (The Hat) Walker . . . because he was constantly reaching for the bill of his cap. This was not to dress up a spitter—Walker hung his Hat in the outfield—but to relieve jitters. The brother of Dixie Walker, The Hat and a Cat (Harry Breechen) played together on a Dr. Seussian Cardinal team of the 1940s.

(Slapsy) Maxie Rosenbloom . . . because this pugilist fought with the perseverance, grace and relative success of the side of beef that Sylvester (Sly) Stallone pummeled in *Rocky*.

John (Champ) Summers . . . because, when he was a homely newborn, this thoroughly mediocre ballplayer's dad thought he looked as if he had just gone 15 rounds with Joe Louis.

THE MISS NOMER PAGEANT

The contestants have paraded before the judges in ill-fitting nicknames, and the finalist deemed to have the most ridiculously inapt moniker will be crowned (with a wrong-sized tiara) Miss Nomer. But first the runners-up:

The Los Angeles Lakers. Wonderfully definitive when the team played in the Land of 10,000 Lakes. But the name lost all significance when they left Minneapolis for the Land of 10,000 Flakes.

The Los Angeles Dodgers. The team was named for trolley-dodging Brooklynites, and a move to Freewayland should have been accompanied by a name change. (The City of Angels also kept the Rams' nickname when that team moved from Cleveland, the Raiders from Oakland and the Clippers from San Diego. The "City of Angels" tag probably wasn't L.A.'s originally, either.)

The Seattle SuperSonics. Boeing's headquarters are in Seattle, and the company was going to build supersonic transports there. Congress nixed funding for the SST shortly after the new franchise selected the name. The NBA already had Nix, or something similar, and so they remained the Sonics.

And the winner is—our new Miss Nomer—ladies and gentlemen . . . The Utah Jazz. A noteworthy nickname in New Orleans, it doesn't play in Salt Lake City, where there's plenty of honky, but very little tonk.

Stan Mikita (Mouse) . . . because Chicago Stadium often rocked with the chant of "M-I-K, I-T-A, M-O-U-S-E—Mikita Mouse." When the Soviet premier visited *Mickey* Mouse at Disneyland in 1961, there was some talk among Blackhawk fans of showing goodwill by changing their hero's nickname to Stan Mikita (Khrushchev). Alas, Chris Berman (see p.3) was but a child at the time.

(Invisi-) Bill Cartwright . . . because of his history of injuries and timid play in New York, where this Knicks forward was also called Mr. Bill, not out of respect, but in reference to the fragile clay figure on "Saturday Night Live" who got maimed every week.

The Halfway House . . . because Rene Lachemann gave transient players an opportunity to salvage their careers while he managed the Seattle Mariners. When Gaylord Perry won 10 games and Al Cowens and Todd Cruz combined for 135 RBIs in 1982, Lachemann heaped praise on his scrap heap. "The Halfway House did some damage," he'd say.

Lloyd (Load) Moore . . . because this round roundballer was more concerned with collecting pounds than 'bounds at Rutgers, where he was also known as Big Daddy Truck. His coaches put him on a conditioning program, hoping Moore would become less; when he didn't, they kicked him off the team.

YOU HAVE TO BE THERE

If you have to ask why Henry Arft was called "Bow Wow," the answer is "Just because." Detailing the derivations of these monikers is like explaining a joke's punch line:

Bob (Ach) Duliba . . . just because. He was given this *wunderbar* nickname as a Cardinal outfielder in the late 1950s.

(What The) Sam Hill. . . just because. His nickname gained popularity at Iowa State, where he was the Cyclones' starting center.

Henry (Bow Wow) Arft . . . just because. A first baseman, Bow Wow was the cat's meow for the Cardinals, circa 1950.

Richie (Zippity) Duda. . . just because. This Polish midfielder for the Chicago Sting was no relation to Jacek (Zippity) Duda, a Pole who played basketball at Providence.

Doug (Eyechart) Gwosdz. . . just because. He played only briefly for the Padres, but there's no truth to the rumor that P. A. announcers threatened to strike if The Chart were made a starter.

Leo (Crystal) Klier . . . just because. Just as all Rhodes have been Dusty and all Cains have been Sugar, so too did this Notre Dame and Fort Wayne guard earn his moniker.

Frantisek (Fran the Man) Musil . . . just because. This Czech hockey player was welcomed to America when he arrived in Minnesota and was immediately named for a certain baseball player of Polish descent.

Gerald (Furniture) Paddio . . . just because. This UNLV guard with the long-distance shooting range suggests the old joke: Q. What's Irish and sits in the backyard? A. Paddy O. Furniture. And it inspired Georgia coach Hugh Durham to crack, "We've got a guy we call Paddio. He throws up enough bricks to build one."

Don (Bird Thou Never) Wert . . . just because. *"Hail to thee blithe spirit, bird thou never wert."* Instead, he wert a Tiger and a Senator. Author Roy Blount, Jr., takes discredit for this one—and for nicknaming Larry (Good Ol') Baugh.

Doug (Eyechart) Gwosdz

Lynbert (Cheese) Johnson . . . just because. This forward had a Whiz of a career at Wichita State.

Johnny (Hippity) Hopp . . . just because. He played first base in St. Louis, a hopping town that was also home to Anthony (Bunny) Brief, who sounds less like a ballplayer than a licensed *Playboy* product.

Eugene (Half-Pint) Rye . . . just because. Gene legally changed his surname to a kind of whiskey after souring on his family label—Mercantelli—before his one season in the Fenway sun.

Frank (Noodles) Zupo . . . just because. Nicknames are good to the very last page of *The Baseball Encyclopedia,* where this fellow immediately follows Bill (Goober) Zuber.

Hercle (Poison) Ivy . . . just because. This former Iowa State hoopster was "string time" strychnine to rivals in Ivy's league.

Virgil (Fire) Trucks . . . just because. His surname invited the nickname, but this reliever's performance also merited it. Remember, Trucks could have just as easily been called Garbage.

RUMBLINGS

Bernie (Boom Boom) Geoffrion . . . because this fab Hab pioneered the slap shot in professional hockey.

Walter (Boom Boom) Beck . . . because of this hurler's lack of pitching prowess. "Beck's nickname was onomatopoetic," writes Golenbock in *Bums*. "The first 'boom' was the ball hitting the bat, and the second 'boom' was the ball hitting the outfield wall."

Norman (Boomer) Esiason . . . because, as a QB-to-be in his mother's womb, he preferred kicking to quarterbacking.

Helmut (Thunderfoot) Dudek . . . because of this MISL fixture's booming shot. With nicknames like these, is it any wonder that soccer hasn't made it in America?

Darryl (Chocolate Thunder) Dawkins . . . because he says so.

THANK GOODNESS DARRYL DAWKINS NEVER PLAYED IN MONTREAL

If he had only been born in the French Quarter and nicknamed then and there, perhaps it wouldn't have sounded so ridiculous. We might even have gotten used to it. As it happened, however, the nurses who helped deliver Daniel Joseph Staub in New Orleans spoke only English, and thus nicknamed the redheaded newborn Rusty. Which is fine, except that twenty-five years later Daniel Joseph would be playing right field for the Montreal Expos, and the French-speaking citizens of that city wouldn't cotton to Staub's *surnom*. In their eyes—and tongue—he was *Le Grand Orange*. The nickname sounded like a French restaurant, and Rusty was fond of food, but it still never had quite the right ring. After three seasons, Staub returned south of the border to play for the

Darryl (Chocolate Thunder) Dawkins

Mets; amazingly, *Le Grand Orange* slipped through customs and gained currency in New York.

Hockey fans in America knew Maurice Richard as The Rocket. And while this Montreal Canadien wasn't as ruthless as some of the league's notorious high-stickers, few would confuse him for a Radio City high-kicker when The Forum crowd hailed *Le Roquette.* The nickname played in either language.

As did William Arthur Johnson's, albeit in a curious way. As a wide receiver and punt returner for the Houston Oilers, he was ahead of his time when it came to footwear. Billy (White Shoes) Johnson was also ahead in the behind department, pioneering an end zone wiggle that was often imitated, never duplicated. In 1981, when he joined the Montreal Alouettes of the Canadian Football League, he found *all* of his teammates wearing white shoes. No matter to the people of Quebec, to whom White Shoes was *Souliers Blancs,* a smooth translation that didn't sound like the English nickname, but still retained its showboat quality. It beat *Le Grand Orange,* anyway.

Ed Tapscott, basketball coach at American University, on one of his players, Longmire Harrison: "We call him Long for short."

BRAND NAMES

Mark (The Pillsbury Doughboy) Aguirre . . . because Chicago's first Fridge weighed 240 pounds in his senior year at DePaul. The elephantine trunks he required as a Dallas Mavericks rookie earned him the name Elephant Drawers—and The Muffin Man, and Fat Daddy, and Ziggy. But now that he's thin, the nicknames aren't in.

Bob (Yellow Pages) Costas . . . because NBC basketball analyst Al McGuire, working his first assignment with play-by-play man Costas, noticed that his diminutive partner couldn't see the action from his courtside seat without the aid of a cushion of phone books.

The Subaru Staff . . . because the Pirates of the mid-1980s have developed a stable of low-salaried, high-ERA pitchers whose medioc-

Mark (The Pillsbury Doughboy) Aguirre

rity doesn't seem to bother management. The staff, in short, is inexpensive and built to stay that way.

Terry (Cadillac) Catledge . . . because, says this NBA forward, "I'm long, black, and lovely."

Terry (Cadillac) Catledge

Billy (The Whopper) Paultz ... because this NBA journeyman center seemed to be put together like an all-the-trimmings burger. During 1985, his final season, Paultz teamed with fellow pale postman Rich Kelley to lead Utah past Houston's Ralph Sampson and Akeem Olajuwon in the playoffs. Forget the Rockets' Twin Towers; Paultz and Kelley, the Jazz's American Towers, were roommates in a Salt Lake City apartment building of that very name.

Calvin (CNN) Muhammad ... because this verbose Redskin, like the Cable News Network, broadcasts twenty-four hours a day.

Mike (Sony) Stenhouse ... because of a string of bases on balls he received as a pinch hitter, this major leaguer was nicknamed for the makers of the Walkman.

Todd (Hewlett-Packard) Kalis ... because this offensive lineman bombarded his Arizona State coaches with hypothetical questions. Like the man in the commercial, he was always asking "What if?"

Bob (Brillo) Tway ... because his wiry hair can double as a scouring pad. Some golfers, who swear it's actually steel wool sprouting on his head, prefer to call Tway SOS. That's free enterprise.

Mike (Titlest Head) Schmidt ... because Philadelphia Phillies teammates believed their third baseman's skin trouble made his face resemble the surface of a golfball. Erstwhile Phillie Pete Rose calls him Herbie Lee, because "he just looks like a Herbie Lee."

Howard (HoJo) Johnson ... because the hotel and restaurant chain that happens to bear his name houses HoJo's Ice Cream Parlors. As a New York Met, however, HoJo had an erratic scoop, and his uneven infield play prompted fans at Shea Stadium to blurt, whenever Johnson made an error, "What flavor was *that?*"

Brent (Allstate) Duhon ... because he was insurance against dropped balls as a wide receiver at Texas. You're in good hands ...

Billy (The Whopper) Paultz

Bold (The Puerto Rican Rolls-Royce) Forbes . . . because Latino jockey Angel (Junior) Cordero thought so highly of this Derby-winning mount.

Amy (Mercedes) Benz . . . because master of the moniker Chris Berman couldn't resist the coinage on an ESPN SportsCenter broadcast. What *is* surprising is that Berman would do so on a sponsored segment of the show called "The Mazda Golf Report."

Luis (Sunoco) Aponte . . . because, rather than putting out the fire, this feckless relief pitcher usually ended up pumping gas on it.

Jody (Timex) Ballard . . . because this former heavyweight, who trained Larry Holmes's sparring partners, would "take a licking and keep on ticking."

THE MENDOZA LINE

Even if it's occasionally a lefthanded one, it *is* nonetheless still a compliment for an athlete to have his real name become a nickname for something else in his society. Walk into a liquor store in Kaunas, Lithuania, for example, and demand a Sabonis, and you'll get their largest bottle of vodka, a tribute to 7'2" Soviet basketball star and local hero Arvidas Sabonis. If you have to get up the next morning, ask for a Misalskis—the name of the star point guard for the local club team. You'll be given the small bottle.

Mario Mendoza conjures up more than a flask of Stolichnaya. His contribution to the English language can be found in baseball. Just as Julius Petri has his commemorative dish, so has Mendoza's name become part of the special shoptalk of his peers, a fitting tribute to one man's unparalleled mediocrity. "The first thing I look for in the Sunday papers is who is below the Mendoza Line," says George Brett, and he is not alone. The Mendoza Line cuts through that treacherous region near the bottom of the agate listing of major league averages. When, say, Max Venable heads south of the Mendoza Line, he isn't going on vacation; rather, his batting average has fallen below .200.

Before Mario's retirement, a player was either above or below the Line depending on whether his average was higher or lower than Mendoza's. Now the reference point is .200, the magical mark with which the shortstop flirted throughout his career. In Mendoza's five seasons in Pittsburgh, he finished above his eponymous line twice and below it three times. At .215, Mendoza's lifetime average is just north of the Line. But it was his performance in the clutch—when he really excelled—that earned him immortality: His career post-season average is .200. Even.

John (Brother Low) Lowenstein . . . because of this utility player's constant proselytizing in the clubhouse. (The "stein" notwithstanding, the boy's a goy.) The spirit didn't move him in Cleveland, however. Nor did much else, for he was known there as Apathy.

Frank (Fuzzy) Zoeller . . . because Frank Urban Zoeller's monogrammed hankies read FUZ.

Kevin (Rodney) Bass . . . because this outfielder lamented the lack of respect he received as a Houston Astro. He kept the handle even after being named National League Player of the Month. "He's still Rodney," said a teammate, "only now it's as in 'Carew'."

Phi Slamma Jamma . . . because the University of Houston Cougars of 1983–84 established a high-flying fraternal order of the court. Thomas Bonk of *The Houston Post* named this frat patrol, whose bylaw, as voiced by brother Benny Anders, was "Take it to the rack and stick it."

BAR GAME #2/MERGERS

When the USFL's Oakland Invaders and Oklahoma Outlaws merged in 1984, staid officials for some reason refused to call the new team the Inlaws. When *you* create the mergers, such oversights can be corrected.

The rules here are simple. Two or more teams merge, and their nicknames are combined to form a new one that's more fun, more appropriate, or both. For instance, the Minnesota Twins and the New York Yankees unite to form the Twinkees; the San Diego Chargers and St. Louis' football Cardinals strike a deal that will make them the Charge Cards.

Don't let the logic tie you down. Teams don't have to be from the same league to merge at your barstool. The NBA's Portland Trail Blazers can join the Ohio Mixers of the Continental Basketball Association as long as the result is the Trail Mixes—the type of health-conscious team that just might cure Bill Walton's foot.

Teams don't have to be playing the same sport to come together, either. Seattle's football team and Cincinnati's baseball club can field an entirely new franchise, whether or not the opposition is prepared to part the Red Seahawks.

No hybrid is too strange. If hockey's St. Louis Blues want to join forces with the Trail Blazers and move the team to Annapolis, that's fine. Fans of the Navy Blue Blazers will be happy they did.

Earvin (Magic) Johnson ... because "Dr. J and the Big E were already taken," said Fred Stabley, Jr., of the *Lansing* (Mich.) *State Journal,* who applied this tag while Johnson was in high school. Not bad for a third choice.

SLEIGHT OF HANDLE

There's a mystical quality about sport's magicians, one that eludes a precise definition. Press a teammate to explain exactly what makes baseball's Rafael Santana a Magic, and you're told, after considerable fidgeting, "He just sort of flips his wand out at the ball." Magic Johnson (does his mother even call him Earvin?) doesn't have a magic touch; his outside shot's the weakest part of his game. But he passes with panache, oozes charisma and smiles that smile—what better way to describe him than Magic?

Earvin (Magic) Johnson

What is the special quality? There are Magics who aren't incredibly talented—Santana is one—and a slew of charismatic players who aren't Magics. Rollie Fingers was one of baseball's best relief pitchers and certainly sported the game's best waxed curlicue mustache. And even though most players have checked into many a cheap motel by the time they reach the bigs, Rollie was never dubbed Magic Fingers.

Lewis Lloyd got it on the playgrounds of Philadelphia, where his nickname, Black Magic, announced his race and his legerdemain with a basketball—and even spawned a Caucasian counterpart, Fran (White Magic) McCaffery. Of all the kids filling it up in Philly, Lloyd had it, and later at Drake University and the NBA, he wanted no one to forget it. When Lloyd and his Drake teammates visited the White House during a swing through Washington, they stood in a receiving line to meet Jimmy Carter. Down the line the President went. "Pop Wright, sir," said one, and Carter moved on. "Tony Watson, sir," said another, and down the line the President went. Then came Lloyd's turn to

Lewis (Black Magic) Lloyd

introduce himself. "Lewis Lloyd, sir," skinheaded Lew said. "The Magic Man, sir."

Tim (Old Second Inning) McCarver . . . because he customarily occupied the john between the first and second inning of *every* game. "He had the most reliable body clock in the world," says Bill (Spaceman) Lee. "We used to set our watches by him."

Marcus (Blackenroe) Allen . . . because his occasional companion on the tennis court, a gent named Kareem Abdul-Jabbar, likens this Raider runner to the pasty husband of Tatum O'Neal.

Leslie (Big Game) Hunter . . . because his last name invited the title, even if his one season in the NBA (1.8 ppg) didn't. Hunter did open fire in the ABA, where he scored in double figures and justified the moniker. Sort of.

FLAMING NAMES

Names are the most bogus part of professional wrestling, and that's no small statement considering how that "sport" has a headlock on schlock. But names are also the most interesting part of pro wrasslin'. Not that someone named Big John Studd isn't taking himself too seriously. The same can be said for, Sterling Golden (that was Hulk Hogan before he became a good guy), The Missing Link, Mr. Wonderful and Adrian Adonis. Comedian Richard Lewis contends that names are the *only* thing one needs to know about professional wrestling. He asks rhetorically: "Don't we know what the outcome will be when Abdullah the Butcher is wrestling Nathan the Bed-Ridden Jew?"

IRONY

(Iron Mike) Ditka . . . because of this NFL coach's mettle as a player. Although when coach Ditka suggested that the entire Packers organization was at fault for Charles (Too Mean) Martin's atomic drop of Bears quarterback Jim McMahon, Milwaukee Mayor Henry Maier said: " 'Iron Mike' must apply to his head."

Dale (Ironhead) Earnhardt . . . because he'd consistently ignore the advice of veteran drivers—including his Ironhearted pop—as a stubborn rookie on the NASCAR circuit.

Ralph (Ironheart) Earnhardt . . . because this manic motorist, who drove like a Bostonian late for an appointment, was the most aggressive driver of his time.

Craig (Ironhead) Heyward . . . because this Pitt football player and school newspaper columnist is a partial native of Pittsburgh; that is, his *head* is a product of the Steel City. It wasn't his prose that left one student in stitches: Ironhead was sidelined with assault and battery charges when a dormmate was beaten around the face with a crutch. "I'm studying juvenile delinquency," quoth the ferrocephalic fullback. "I should know something about it. As a juvenile, I was a delinquent."

Lou (The Iron Horse) Gehrig . . . because his durability was equine, and he wasn't rendered supine through 2,130 games of a distinguished career. Gehrig holds another singular, albeit unenviable, distinction: His real name has become a nickname for the disease that cut him down.

THE OOH CREW

It's late September in the Old Ballyard, and the home team trails the division leader by thirty-six games. Down by five runs in the bottom of

Lou (The Iron Horse) Gehrig

the ninth, the soon-to-be-ex-manager sends Ted Kluless (.138, 0 HR, 3 RBI) in to pinch hit. A low rumble rises from the 1,217 masochists attending. The rumble becomes a thunderclap of boos as frustrated fans, seeing another season gone bad, air their hostility. Then, invariably, the radio announcer, hired by the front office to dispense positive public relations, says amid the clamor: "The faithful here are yelling 'Kluuu-uuu!' as Kluless steps to the plate!"

The New York Mets lost 120 games in 1962, giving their fans ample reason to boo them. Instead, the crowds were content to chant "Choo Choo! Choo Choo!" as homage to catcher Clarence (Choo Choo) Coleman. Even when Choo Choo didn't play, Mets fans showed their affection by calling his nickname. Wait a minute. Were they *really* saying "Choo Choo"? Says Coleman himself: "Yeah, Bub." (Of course, Coleman responded to *every* question with "Yeah, Bub.")

Oklahoma basketball player Darryl (Choo) Kennedy was only half as bold as Coleman in choosing an "ooh" name that always sounds like "boo" when a crowd croons it. When basketball fans in Milwaukee call for Brew, they're not always hailing a vendor selling the city's most celebrated product. They may be imploring the Bucks' coach to put center Randy Breuer into the lineup.

Many more athletes, including UCLA point guard Jerome (Pooh) Richardson, have pooh-poohed more conventional nicknames in favor of one that goes "ooh," too. Consider: One Boo wasn't enough to cover 310-pound Curtis (Boo Boo) Rouse, an offensive lineman for the Minnesota Vikings. Two Boos were too many for Anthony Bowie, however, who preferred the singular Boo as his nickname at Oklahoma (where Boo teamed with Choo).

LUGGAGE TAGS

Leroy (Satchel) Paige . . . because, it was originally thought, his feet were as big as suitcases. But Satch himself attributes it to his days as a porter in Alabama.

James (American Tourister) Donaldson . . . because "His head's as big as a suitcase," says rival NBA center Darryl Dawkins. He's also well-traveled.

Twins manager Billy Gardner, on outfielder *(Downtown) Darrell Brown,* who hit one homer in 519 at bats: "That must be an awfully small town."

JO JO WHITE AND THE SEVEN DWARFS

Consider Glenn (Doc) Rivers, Eric (Sleepy) Floyd and Harold (Happy) Hairston. Are these guys proof positive that dwarfs can play in the NBA? Not necessarily. But they're enough of an invitation to indulge in a bit of whimsy. Here's a supporting cast:

At the guards, Micheal Ray (Dopey) Richardson and John (Sneezy) Lucas, for their travails with drugs.

At forward, Moses (Grumpy) Malone. Yes, we know he's a center. But being easygoing and all, Mo would be more than happy to make the switch.

Darryl (Bashful) Dawkins, who has bashed a few backboards in his time, would help hold together the middle.

And, to call the shots: Joseph (Jo Jo) White. He didn't want to be your average Joe.

Jet (The Cosmetics Kid) Pilot . . . because this horse, the 1947 Kentucky Derby champion, was owned by make-up millionaire Elizabeth Arden.

Darrel (Kool FM) Akerfelds . . . because one spring training this pitcher's earned run average hit 94.5.

(Peddlin') Jay Meddlin . . . because this leg-pumping wheelie-popper was an early bicycle motocross (BMX) champion.

THE ALL WHO-NEEDS-A-NICKNAME BOWLING TEAM

Five Professional Bowlers Association figures who will never need a nickname:

Dale Strike
Billy Block
Dave Frame
Curv Rohler
Brad Bohling

Glenn (Fireball) Roberts . . . because this driver's stock car seemed to be an incendiary blur as he pursued new speed records around the track. In 1964, he died in a fiery crash.

Steve (Psycho) Lyons . . . because he's a psychopath on the basepaths. As sportscaster Tony Kubek has said of baseball's Norman Bates: "He's one of those guys where, if you're a first-base coach, you say 'Gimme a lasso.' "

Roberto (Hands of Stone) Duran . . . because he won bout after bout with his mason's touch. That was, of course, before *Manos de Piedra* wanted *"no mas."*

Pearce (What's the Use?) Chiles . . . because this exasperated Athletic rang in the new century by creating a new position, that of futility infielder. Chiles batted .329 in his rookie season, but dipped to .220 in 1900, his second and last gig in the bigs.

MARQUEE NAMES

The Killer Tomatoes . . . because the cardinal-clad defense at Santa Clara University was as vicious as the vegetables in *Attack of the Killer Tomatoes.* You say "tomato," and linebacker coach Ron DeMonner will say their motto: "We'll catch you, eat you, burp twice and keep going." To the chagrin of a nearby Del Monte plant, efforts to install a Ketchup Offense at Santa Clara were squashed.

Shelton (The Amityville Horror) Jones . . . because this St. John's star is from Amityville, N.Y., home of the haunted house of so much ballyhoo. He's also frighteningly versatile.

Kevin (E.T.) Moley . . . because he had a string of eighth- and tenth-round knockouts, executed while wearing eight- and ten-ounce gloves. The late Paddy Flood, the manager who tagged Moley, was asked if his fighter had heard from Steven Spielberg.

Steve (Psycho) Lyons

"Who?" Flood asked.
"The guy who made the movie."
"What movie?"
"*E.T.*!"
"Never saw it," said Flood. "But we're fighting this guy Spiegel-
    berger next."

John (Hondo) Havlicek . . . because of this former Celtic's passion for Western novels and an early resemblance to John Wayne. So branded by Ohio State mate Mel Nowell.

Steve (Claude Rains) McCatty . . . because he was in Oakland's starting rotation, yet pitched so infrequently he seemed to be The Invisible Man.

The Marks Brothers . . . because the Dolphins' duo of wide receivers, messieurs Duper and Clayton, share the same first name. Receiving lesser marks: Such nicknames as Marks of Excellence and The Magic Markers.

(The Marks Brothers)

Reggie (Freddy) Miller . . . because this UCLA star, who has been called "sissy" by his All-America sister Cheryl (really), wears his hair closely cropped, like Freddy Krueger, the alopecic villain of the *Nightmare on Elm Street* movies. "Bald intimidates people," says Miller. "Freddy is mean, real mean."

Vinnie (Vincent Priceless) Testaverde . . . 'cause this able 'Cane quarterback and Heisman Trophy winner was invaluable to the University of Miami.

RAMBO

If Sylvester Stallone followed a nickname trend in his first movie (see Sugars and Rockys, p. 47), he certainly *set* one with *Rambo: First Blood, Part II*. That flick, whose hero, John J. Rambo, was a brooding, one-man army, was a boom at the box office *and* the talk of many a locker room.

They saw it in St. Louis, where Cardinals ordained Jack Clark, a new arrival with a dark countenance, Rambo.

They also saw it in Philadelphia, where Phils pitcher John Denny drilled San Diego's Tim Flannery in the head and later charged the offending hit-batsman at third base. Denny became Rambo. Later, Phillie administrator Tony Siegle would lay gastronomical waste to a Wrigley Field coldcut spread, and be dubbed Crambo by Denny himself.

To be sure, some women, Soviets and Asian-Americans were offended by *Rambo,* but as a nickname, anyway, it was an equal-opportunity moniker. Ray Salters, a 6'2" 220-pound basketball player for Cleveland State, may not exactly have been Jackie Robinson, but he *was* sport's first Black Rambo.

The Three Stooges . . . because Rick (Moe) Dempsey, Todd (Curly) Cruz and Rich (Larry) Dauer of the 1983 Orioles were a trio of screwballs who couldn't hit the *nyuck-nyuck-nyuck*leball, or anything else. Dauer's .235 was the highest average among the Stooges. "I don't consider myself a .235 hitter," Larry was quick to point out. "Although I *did* hit .235." Moe, of course, would be the World Series MVP that October.

The Broderick Crawford Highway Patrol . . . because Broderick Thompson and Crawford Ker, guards on the Dallas offensive line, got out and practiced a little enforcement during Cowboys sweeps.

Steve (Michael Jackson) Sax . . . because this second baseman and his nick-namesake both wear a glove on one hand for no apparent reason.

Steve (Stevie Wonder) Stroughter . . . because, as Rene Lachemann, his manager in Milwaukee, said, "Every time they hit the ball to him you wonder what's gonna happen."

The Four Tops . . . because Western Kentucky's four frontcourt seniors—6'10" Tellis Frank, 6'9" Kannard Johnson, 6'8" Clarence Martin and 6'6" Bryan Asberry—hit the high notes for the 1986–87 Hilltoppers.

GOOD LINES

Bob & Carol & Ted & Dallas . . . because *Bob & Carol & Ted & Alice* was in movie houses when Bobby Orr, Carol Vadnais, Ted Green and Dallas Smith were starring as a line for the Boston Bruins.

The Gag Line . . . because of a bent for choking or practical joking? *Non.* The Rangers relied on this group—led by Rod Gilbert—to score a *g*oal *a g*ame.

The French Connection . . . because the Buffalo Sabres' line of Rene Roberts, Richard Martin and Gilbert Perrault had a distinctive francophone sound to it.

ANSWERS TO QUESTIONS THAT MAY HAVE OCCURRED TO YOU

Q: What was Early Wynn's full given name?
A: Early Wynn

Q: How many fingers did Mordecai (Three Finger) Brown have on the hand that earned him his nickname?
A: Four.

Q: How many dingers did Frank (Home Run) Baker hit in 1913, his most productive season?
A: Twelve.

Q: What was the ethnic background of Bobby (The Greek) DelGreco, the Pirate outfielder of the 1950s?
A: Italian.

 Walter (The Truth) Berry . . . because of this New York high school and schoolyard legend's doctrinal manner of play. When, after his junior season at St. John's, he made assurances he'd stay for his senior year but proceeded to enter the NBA Draft, he became known among Big Apple cynics as Walter (The Lie) Berry.

(Mean) Joe Greene . . . because no other adjective quite fit the way this Pittsburgh Steelers defensive end played the game during the 1970s, and comported himself in general, except when he made the occasional Coca-Cola commercial. The North Texas State defense he played with was known as the Mean Green, while Greene was just plain Joe; but when he hit the big leagues, NTSU began using Mean Green for its athletic teams just as often as Eagles.

(Large) Ira Harge . . . because, at 6'9", 225 pounds, this ABA journeyman *was*. Harge pioneered this style of nickname, becoming Large at New Mexico while Joe Greene was still a pre-Mean teen.

Edward (Porky) Oliver . . . because he lugged 225 pounds around the links. His girth wasn't the only part of his legacy of excess; Oliver is still remembered for taking a sixteen on the 222-yard 16th hole at Cypress Point during the 1954 Crosby.

TEN BAD RING NAMES

10. *The Orchid Man.* Georges Carpentier was thinking of The Orkin Man, exterminator and TV spokesman for the pest control company, when he mistakenly took this name as his own.

9. *The Hard Rock From Down Under.* Never, Tom Heeney, end a ring name with three prepositions.

8. *The Terre Haute Terror.* With all due apologies to Bud Taylor, the only Terror ever to pass through Terre Haute wears number 33 for the Boston Celtics.

7. *The Fargo Express.* Billy Petrolle had the misfortune of hailing from the one city that strikes less fear in the heart than Terre Haute.

6. *The Basque Woodchopper.* More than a ring name, Paulino Uz-

cudun needed a given name with fewer syllables.

5. *The Philadelphia Dancing Master.* Arthur Murray *boxed?* No, it was Tommy Loughran who used this one.

4. *The Manly Marine.* Gene Tunney's ring name *and* the name of the movie they were showing at your bachelor party.

3. *The Scotch Wop.* Johnny Dundee may have had Scotch in his ring name, but we know he never *really* had a belt. Championship, that is.

2. *The Garrulous Gob.* For those who don't speak Redundant Alliteration, Jack Sharkey's ring name means "The Talkative Mouth."

1. *The Tall Tower of Gorgonzola.* Poor Primo Carnera. Gorgonzola is hardly the ideal substance to be a tall tower of.

HARDWARE

Jack (Hacksaw) Reynolds . . . because, after his Tennessee team had lost 38–0 to Ole Miss, Reynolds bought a hacksaw and twelve blades on sale at a Knoxville K-Mart and proceeded to saw an abandoned car in half, slicing it right behind the door jam between the front and back seats. The task took eight hours, but Reynolds would get great mileage out of it. (The nickname, not the car.)

Fred (The Hammer) Williamson . . . because this Kansas City Chiefs defensive back's favorite weapon was "a blow to the head perpendicular to the earth's latitude." When not hammering receivers or syntax, Williamson was woofing; before Super Bowl I he vowed to end Green Bay receiver Carroll Dale's career. "We call him the Tackhammer," said one unimpressed Packer. "He doesn't hit very hard." Indeed, Green Bay guard Gale Gillingham hammered Williamson on a second-half sweep, knocking him out cold. The Hammer was last seen—surprise—in Hollywood, where the license plates on his car read DA HAMMA.

Dave (The Hammer) Schultz . . . because this charter member of the Broad Street Bullies, those forechecking, sorechecking Philadelphia Flyers teams, was always atop the penalty stats.

Len (Nails) Dykstra . . . because that's what he's as tough as. He also hammered a few in the coffins of the Astros and Red Sox during the 1986 post-season.

John (Buzzsaw) Gant . . . because the ball he bowls makes its way down the alley with more revolutions than a fledgling Central American democracy, leaving the pins in a heap of dust.

BASKETBALLISTICS

In basketball, where the jump shot is lovingly referred to as the J, exceptional shooters tend to earn firearm-related nicknames. Each of the players here can or could really shoot the J, except for those who played in an earlier era. (Because the set shot was never known as the S, suffice it to say that the oldies could just plain really shoot.)

(Pistol) Pete Maravich. His unconscionable gunning drove countless coaches to lobby for stricter handgun legislation.

Roger (The Rifle) Strickland. At 6′5″, he's the same size as the Pistol, yet has a higher-caliber nickname. How come? After all, The Rifle scored two points in his entire professional career. That's a mere half-court hook for Maravich.

John (Shotgun) Hargis. Despite being sawed off at 6′2″, Shotgun had four productive seasons in professional basketball.

Jack (The Shot) Foley. A beautiful nickname—succinct, expressive . . . and eventually erroneous. Perhaps because The Shot shot the lights out at Holy Cross, he was a Shot in the dark in his one NBA season, when he averaged five points per game.

(Sonar) Joe Hassett. Named for the system that can detect objects underwater from great distances, Sonar was fond of submerging the basketball from afar. His career was given new life when the NBA adopted the three-point line.

George (Radar) Stone. Also named for his great range, this forward lasted four seasons in the ABA before his shooting touch began to take after his surname.

George (The Blind Bomber) Glamack. A moderate scorer during the

(Pistol) Pete Maravich

1940s, Glamack could have been the game's *worst* shooter and still have kept this nickname.

Ralph (Buckshot) O'Brien. An exceptionally poor shooter, Buckshot's spray was all over the court in Indianapolis and Baltimore during the early 1950s.

Harvey's Wallbangers . . . because "We keep bangin' 'em off the walls," said Cecil Cooper, first baseman for the slugging Milwaukee Brewers who won the 1982 pennant under peachy Harvey Kuenn.

Zack (No Slack) Trueblood . . . because of the lack of slack this Californian gave rivals on the basketball court. Trueblood shouldn't have cut himself quite so much slack in the classroom; his career ended at New Jersey's Monmouth College in 1984 with academic problems.

Charles (Casey) Stengel . . . because, before this baseball fixture began embarking on his unpredictable soliloquies, he was known primarily for hailing from K.C. With age, he became The Ol' Perfesser.

Keith (End Zone) Jones . . . because this Nebraska ball carrier, who ran 40 yards in 4.3 seconds, could get there, and frequently did.

THE SHOT HEARD 'ROUND THE WORLD

It wasn't just a game. It was an event, one that required a title with which to give those born later a feel for exactly what happened on October 3, 1951. The voice of Russ Hodges didn't hurt, either: *"There's a long drive . . . it's gonna be . . . I believe . . . The Giants win the pennant! The Giants win the pennant! The Giants win the pennant! The Giants win the pennant!"*

The Shot Heard 'Round the World had less to do with Concord, Mass., than it did with Conquered Dodgers. The Miracle at Coogan's Bluff had nothing to do with turning water into wine, and everything to do with turning whines into wishes-come-true for New York Giants fans.

Charles (Casey) Stengel

Bobby Thomson fired his round in Game 3 of a three-game playoff series that decided the pennant—a playoff made necessary when the Giants gained thirteen and a half games on Brooklyn between August and October, tying Dem Bums for foist in the National League. Trailing 4–2 with one out and two on in the bottom of the ninth, Thomson sent Ralph (Hawk) Branca's second pitch into the Polo Grounds' left-field bleachers. The celebrated Shot, according to the New York *Daily News,* Heard 'Round the World. The Miracle at Coogan's Bluff.

The *News* was barely hyperbolic. On that day, the world indeed seemed like the one mapped out in *The New Yorker* cartoon, in which the city covers three-quarters of the globe. Bobby Thomson wasn't to be remembered by his nickname—the Staten Island Scot—but for the homer that scotched the Dodgers.

HOUSEHOLD NAMES

Jaime (The Piano) Cardriche . . . because this Oklahoma State lineman goes 6'9" and 395 pounds, and is tightly strung.

Vinnie (The Microwave) Johnson . . . because, says NBA rival Danny Ainge, "He heats up so fast."

THE FRIDGE

The nicknames and legend began at Clemson, where William (The Refrigerator) Perry packed away more groceries than a bagboy on commission (including *a case and a half* of beer, and Lord knows how many pretzels, in savoring one particularly sweet victory). When he reported to his first Bears camp at 330 pounds plus, defensive coordinator Buddy Ryan called him "a wasted draft pick," and Perry's new teammates called him Biscuit because, they said, "he's a biscuit away from 350." But The Fridge, ever conscious that the waist is a terrible thing to mind, simply went about making the sporting world safe for appliances. After Perry spent his post-Super Bowl off-season shilling for more products than Mary Lou Retton, teammates taped another nickname to The Refrigerator: William (The Endorser) Perry. And now they call him Avalanche because, as John Madden explains, "When he takes off his t-shirt, one happens."

Johnny Carson, on football players in England: "They're not real intimidating. Instead of William (The Refrigerator) Perry, they have Colin (The Tea Cozy) Dimsdale."

William (The Fridge) Perry

Joe (The Defroster) Milinichik . . . because of a hit this 308-pound North Carolina State offensive lineman applied to a certain defensive appliance in a game against Clemson. Playing opposite William Perry, The Defroster's hit disconnected The Fridge from his helmet.

Nate (The Kitchen) Newton . . . because he came to his first Cowboys training camp fully equipped with 332 pounds. Said Randy White, on his first visit to The Kitchen: "He looks more like the whole floor plan to me." His brother is Tim *(The Icebox)* Newton.

James (The Heat) Kinchen . . . because this middleweight advised, in his own inimitable body language, "If you can't stand The Heat, get out of the Kinchen."

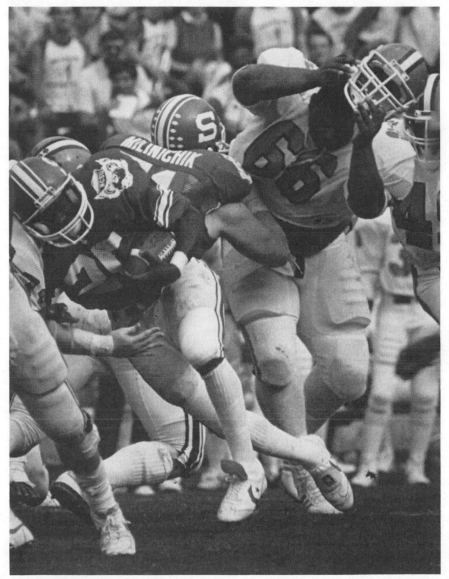

Joe (The Defroster) Milinichik

Eddie (Meat Cleaver) Weaver . . . because of his nasty visage and unpleasant demeanor. And demeanor he got, de better he played as a Georgia defensive lineman.

Bill (The Singer Throwing Machine) Singer . . . because of this pitcher's endurance. His won-lost record, on the other hand, was only sew-sew over two decades.

RHYMED COUPLETS

The Louie and Bouie Show. It ran at Syracuse, where the leading Orangemen on the basketball court were Louis Orr and Roosevelt Bouie.

The Bernie and Ernie Show. Premiered when Bernard King and Ernie Grunfeld were at Tennessee, it reran when they became teammates on the Knicks. Though they shared the marquee, Bernie always had a bigger and better role.

Lo-rilla and Co-rilla. Lorenzo Charles and Cozell McQueen were so fond of Go-rilla dunks at North Carolina State that, Lo and behold, Charles capped their 1983 championship with one.

Hobble and Wobble. Erstwhile Redskin quarterback Sonny Jurgensen was decrepit, and the guy behind him on the depth chart, Billy Kilmer, couldn't throw a spiral.

Rags and Pags. Yankees Dave Righetti and Mike Pagliarulo. Yogi Berra couldn't spell, much less pronounce, his third baseman's name, which is why he always wrote Pags on the lineup card.

Wicks and Sticks. The Rutgers Lady Knights were a women's basketball power during the 1980s with a frontline of Sue Wicks and Regina (Sticks) Howard.

Utah Jazz coach Frank Layden, on his basketball days coming up in Brooklyn: "We had a lot of nicknames—Scarface, Blackie, Toothless. And those were just the cheerleaders."

(The Bernie and Ernie Show)

YOU CAN CALL ME COOL, OR YOU CAN CALL ME J. C., OR . . .

Calvin Coolidge Julius Caesar Tuskahoma McLish's nickname is listed in *The Official Encyclopedia of Baseball* as "Cal."

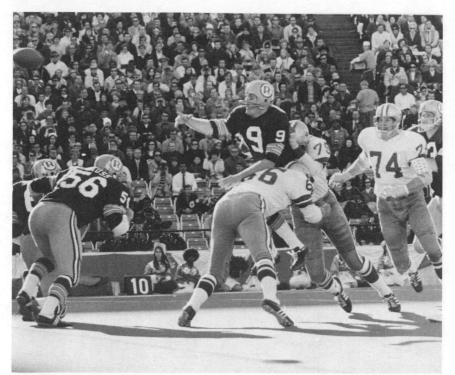

Sonny Jurgensen (Hobble)

🏀 **Bill (The Hill) McGill** . . . because opponents had a tough time getting over or around this Seton Hall star's 6'9" and 225-pound frame. A melodic nickname that joins baseball's Emil (Hillbilly) Bildilli as a triumph of the *ill.*

⚾ **Mike (No Bo) Diaz** . . . because this Phils prospect couldn't catch like Bo (No Relation) Diaz. Glenn Wilson turned in that scouting report when he pronounced: "He's no Bo."

🏀 **Alex (Flick) English** . . . because, as a kid, he played basketball languidly, as if afflicted with some sort of disease. "Flicked," they called him, and Flick would stick even after English became the smooth poet laureate of the NBA.

⛳ **Juan (Chi Chi) Rodriguez** . . . because baseball was this golfer's first love. "I got my name from Chi Chi Flores, who played Class A ball

Billy Kilmer (Wobble)

in Puerto Rico." Says Rodriguez, "I was his biggest fan. We had Roberto Clemente on that team. They used him as a pinch runner."

OWIN' PAINS

Former Bengals quarterback Jack Thompson, born in Tutuwila, Samoa, was nicknamed The Throwin' Samoan. Orioles hurler Sammy Stewart, from Swannanoa, Georgia, was—you catch on quick!—The Throwin' Swannanoan.

TIPS TO REMEMBER

Former Speaker of the House Thomas (Tip) O'Neill, Jr., swung a mean gavel, but that isn't why he was nicknamed for James (Tip) O'Neill, a St. Louis Browns outfielder of the 1880s. Spake the Speaker: "That was the only year in baseball that a base on balls counted as a base hit. O'Neill would get up and foul them off until he got a base on balls. The Irish loved him. There's a Tip O'Neill everywhere now, but he's the original Tip O'Neill."

Frank (Tug) McGraw . . . because this pitcher/cartoonist/cut-up had a habit as a toddler of constantly yanking on things.

The 46 Defense . . . because Doug Plank wore that number on his Bears uniform when Buddy (Whatsizname?) Ryan installed the system responsible for Chicago's victory in Super Bowl XX. "The only reason it was the 46," explained Bears coach Mike Ditka, "was because the coach couldn't think of the player's name."

(Dollar) Bill Bradley . . . because this parsimonious banker's son became a money player at Princeton and with the Knicks, entered politics and may someday have his face on a dollar bill. Walt Hazzard paid him the ultimate compliment during the 1964 Olympics, when he sang the praises of "The White O."

Alvin (Titanic) Thompson . . . because, whether by knocking the ball into the cup from twenty-five feet with his instep, or by using more orthodox means, this legendary hustler from Texas was going to sink it. (He was also of ample girth.)

CECIL THE DIESEL

"Playing middle linebacker," erstwhile Buccaneer Cecil (The Diesel) Johnson once observed, "is like walking through a lions' cage in a three-piece pork chop suit." Cecil, a.k.a. Big Daddy, gave vent to job-related stress by coining biting nicknames for his Tampa Bay team-mates.

As a result, offensive lineman Ray Snell became Martian. "He must be one," reasoned Cecil. "He's black and got green eyes. They sent him down on a mission. Got to dye his eyes."

Two of Cecil's less comely colleagues, both of whom shall remain anonymous (until you spot their pictures in the program), are Moon Crater Face and Barney Rubble Face. Eugene Sanders, a 6'3", 285-pound tackle with a shock of hair that tends to stand at attention, is Godzilla. Not Godzilla Face? "Hell no," says Cecil. "You see how big he is? I call him Godzilla straight up. Ain't no 'Face' *in* it."

Nose tackle Dave Logan, he of the large feet, answers to Sasquatch. "He may not be the craziest guy I know," Sasquatch says of Cecil, "but he's definitely in the playoffs."

COLLEGE BASKETBALL'S ALL–BABY TALK TEAM

Jerome (Pooh) Richardson, UCLA.
Darryl (Choo) Kennedy, Oklahoma.
Greg (Boo) Harvey, St. John's.
Eric (Boo Boo) Brent, James Madison.
Karl (Boobie) James, Georgetown.

Honorary Captain: *Glenn Puddy,* Southern Methodist. No nickname, but how 'bout that surname? Puddy (rhymes with Goody), as in "I tawt I taw a Puddy-tat."

Storm (Cy Clone) Davis . . . because of this Baltimore pitcher's early resemblance to three-time Cy Young winner Jim Palmer. The original Denton (Cy) Young, incidentally, earned his nickname because he threw with the force of a cyclone. All of which makes Storm, whose real name is George, considerably less powerful.

Cornelius (Connie Mack) McGillicuddy . . . because life, like the space on a lineup card, was too short for his real name. A.k.a. Slats/ and The Tall Tactician.

ELECTRIC 'TO-STARS

Catch Wilt Chamberlain talking about the *'to* and he won't be pointing to one of the appendages on his perpetually bare feet. The Dipper's *'to* is the ghetto, where nicknames are a prevalent part of basketball and, hence, a prevalent part of life. Those in the *'to* most agile with a *rock* (basketball) establish a *rep* (reputation) which will guarantee them action in a *run* (a full-court game) whenever they want. From such runs flow nicknames, mythic lore and honest-to-God street legends.

Three of the most hallowed playgrounders ever to lace up a pair of Cons were Jackie Jackson, Herman Knowings and Earl Manigault. Each player carries with him an amaaazing story all his own, stories told over and over by those in New York who saw 'em play. Who needs a VCR when you have urban oral history?

(Sidecar) Jackie Jackson carried the rock on his hip like so many school books as he drove to the hoop, ultimately pulling the ball from the "sidecar" and taking a jam. Playing in the days when a phone call cost a dime, Sidecar was always ready to chat, for he could pick a quarter off the top of the backboard, and, with superhuman hang time and a little common courtesy, leave fifteen cents change.

Anyone who saw Herman Knowings ascend knows why he was called The Helicopter. Anyone who's heard this story knows why, too:

Playing a game in the Rucker League, Harlem's prestigious pro-am summer tournament, The 'Copter found himself playing defense in the lane when an opponent head-faked him off terra firma. He remained aloft, hovering—until his man was called for three seconds.

And there was The Goat, a Harlem institution to rival the Apollo. When Earl Manigault parted the crowd by a wire fence and walked into the schoolyard, even the youngest youngbloods knew it was he—Manigault, or "Nannygoat," or "Goat." Though his career ended when The Goat got on The Horse (or The H—heroin), drugs didn't stop him from counseling kids and cultivating his own urban garden of talent. Describing a certain prodigy he had taken under his wing, Goat said, "He's the baddest dude in the world. He can tap dunk on a guy 6'9". I call him 'God.' "

NATURAL PHENOMENAMES

Len (Frosty) Bias . . . because this Maryland forward was so cool. The sad irony is that Frosty died of cocaine intoxication two days after he was drafted number one by the Celtics in 1986.

Joe (Foggy) Altobelli . . . because his players thought this erstwhile Baltimore and San Francisco manager a little thick and not too bright. Said one Oriole pitcher, who thought Altobelli had yanked him prematurely: "It was just like San Francisco. About the seventh inning, the Fog rolled in."

Joel (Sunshine) Katz . . . because this career benchwarmer at Syracuse came to the upstate New York tundra from Puerto Rico.

Benny (Eclipse) Ayala . . . because, says this journeyman, "I'm an eclipse player. You don't see me very often."

PEARLS

The first oyster was pried open on a south Philadelphia playground. There, bobbing and whirling and teaching some old basketball new tricks, was V. Earl Monroe, a Pearl more lustrous than Bailey, destined to explode more than Harbor, and the first and best-known Pearl in sport. Sure, his middle name helped—*Vernon* the Pearl doesn't exactly sing—but it was his ability to leave defenders sans jockstrap that made him the charter member of his nickname genus.

Unlike the pretenders who went by Babe after Ruth retired, Dwayne (Pearl) Washington is filling Monroe's vacated oyster shell quite capably. (Monroe was *The* Pearl, but Washington, the former Brooklyn and Syracuse star now in the NBA, doesn't use the article; he's just Pearl.) He came to be known as Pearl (Dwayne) Washington, so much a part of his real name was his nickname; and Syracuse teammates even took to nicknaming him again, as though Pearl was his *given* name. His Orange backcourt partner, Rafael (Raf) Addison, once sauntered over to a salad bar and impaled five black olives on the tips of the fingers of one hand. "What's this?" he asked, holding up his hand. Pointing to his friend's elliptical skull, Raf said, "Pearl, five times over!" After that, he was Pearl (Olive Head) Washington to his college buddies. And, occasionally, Pearl (Fat Butt) Washington.

Nestled between Monroe and Washington in basketball's string of Pearls is one Pearl Moore, who set the all-time, either-sex, collegiate scoring record in amassing 4,061 points at South Carolina's Francis Marion College. Going on to star for the New York Stars of the NDWBL, the Now-Defunct Women's Basketball League, Moore scored a third of her team's points in one game in a 96–95 win. Reading the totals on WCBS-TV in New York, sportscaster Len (No Relation to Chris) Berman couldn't resist coining a complimentary new nickname. He reverently referred to the 5'7" guard as Pearl the Earl.

Steve (Tooter) Braun . . . because Braun's father was called Tootsie. "I didn't look like a Tootsie," Braun said, long before widespread cocaine use in baseball would make his eventual moniker hazardous. "So I became a Tooter."

Earl (The Pearl) Monroe

Dwayne (Pearl) Washington

(Two-Ton) Tony Galento . . . because, by conservative estimates, he weighed that much. He was also called The Battling Barkeep, and indeed this heavyweight chump's best shots were those he served saloon patrons. Galento would quit the sweet science and become a successful professional wrestler.

Ernie (Pop) Lewis . . . because this former Providence guard has a brother called Snap and a sister called Crackle.

Pearl (The Earl) Moore

Terry (Orville Moody) Kennedy . . . because of this catcher's touchy temperament.

Michael (The Silk) Olajide . . . because this middleweight and Michael Jackson look-alike moves smoothly in the ring, and outside it, where he's a slick dresser and part-time model.

Dennis (Oil Can) Boyd . . . because oil is what they call beer in Meridian, Mississippi, where this pitcher grew up. Boyd's childhood friend Paps (" 'cause he only drinks Paps Blue Ribbon") nicked the Can after watching sixteen-year-old Dennis pound about four quarts one evening. Many would like to see the Can can his hotdog antics. Pete Rose calls him Trash Can, but Boyd isn't about to put a lid on anything. "I've got color. I've got character. I'm the Caaaaaaaan," he says. To Gene Mauch, he's Dipstick. Dipsticks and stones don't bother the Can, but sticks in the *mud* do. Ronald (Dutch) Reagan signed a picture "to Dennis Boyd." Explained the Duke of Oil: "He wanted to sign it 'to the Can,' but they're pretty conservative at the White House."

John (Junior) McEnroe . . . because his father is John McEnroe, Sr. On those rare occasions when Junior isn't baring his pearly whites at umpires, he's known as Mac the Nice.

BAR GAME #3/CORPORATE TAKEOVERS

Sports in America have become almost as commercialized as Christmas in America. Everyone knows that Michael Jordan wears *those* shoes, and that Jim McMahon favors *these* headbands. And we're at least pretty sure we know what brand of underwear Jim Palmer is sporting on any given day. As corporations look increasingly toward professional athletes to promote their products, one man lends foresight.

He's Fran DiBacco of Turnersville, N.J., who suggested in *The Sporting News* that Joan Kroc, widow of McDonald's founder Ray Kroc and owner of the San Diego Padres, just might purchase Denver's NBA franchise and make them the McNuggets. He also speculated that General Motors would buy the hockey Devils, turning them into the

New Jersey DeVilles. By buying a team and changing its nickname ever so subtly, corporations could sneak in free advertising each night on the evening sportscast.

Such takeovers need not be limited to big business, however. Individuals can purchase teams as a means of expressing themselves, as Henry Winkler could do in the Bay Area. The Fonz just might purchase the American League team there, and rename them the Oakland Aaaaaaay's. If deposed Philippines president Ferdinand Marcos wants to seek solace in the States by wresting control of the football team in Foxboro, Mass., they could become the New England Expatriates.

The various professional leagues should guard against such unsavory takeovers. Beware if Radio City Music Hall, Gillette, Sherwin Williams, Mikhail Gorbachev and Ticketron should seek to buy existing NBA franchises. We could end up hearing this on the 11 o'clock news: "The Houston Rockettes defeated the New York Nicks, the L. A. Lacquers downed the New Jersey Nyets, while the Boston Sell Tix were idle tonight."

HAIL PALE

Greg (The Great White Shark) Norman . . . because this white-haired golfer, who has a reputation for being unable to land the big one on the PGA tour, once had much the same problem while fishing in the shark-infested waters off Moreton Bay in his native Australia. "If you had six or seven fish hooked, by the time you'd pull 'em in there would be only two or three left," says Norman, who once grabbed a rifle and opened fire on the sharks circling his boat. "That's how it all started."

Dorrel (Whitey) Herzog . . . because "Johnny Pesky said I looked like a pitcher named Bob Kuzaba," says Herzog. "And they called him the White Rat." Mercifully, White Rat became Whitey. Either way, Herzog was just happy to have a nickname. "My real name is Dorrel Norman Elvert," he says. "I didn't name any of my kids that."

James (The Great White Hope) Jeffries . . . because when Jack Johnson became the first black heavyweight champion in 1910, Jeffries ended a five-year retirement, hoping to regain the crown that was once his. But his racist supporters were disappointed, for the aged Jeffries's boxing ability was, like his skin, only fair, and Johnson beat him badly before the fight was stopped. Most Great White Hopes to follow wouldn't be that Great, and would have little Hope.

END NAMES

Scott (The Terminator) Molina . . . because this superstar triathlete never leads coming out of the water—but always wins it on the run.

Jeff (The Terminator) Reardon . . . because he abruptly ends games once he's freed from the bullpen. Before the Arnold Schwarzenegger flick inspired that tag, he was called Yak-Yak, because, as he said in one of his longer soliloquies, "I don't like to shoot the breeze."

Willie (Ack Ack) Aikens . . . because he stutters.

Tom (The Atom Bomb) Tracey . . . because he wanted it that way. He would correct those who negligently addressed him as Tom (The Bomb) Tracey. "That's the *Atom* Bomb," he would say.

Hernell (Jeep) Jackson . . . because this mobile fellow, before making a name for himself at Texas, El Paso, always used to ride his tricycle around the neighborhood. He died a mysterious death before leaving UTEP.

John (Frenchy) Fuqua . . . because this erstwhile Giant and Steeler fullback had a closetful of clothes, with the French cuffs on the shirts barely the start.

THE TOP TWENTY

Like any professor worth his chalk dust, James (Gilligan!) Skipper busies himself with research in between sociology lectures at Virginia Tech. One of his scholarly treatises, published in the Society for American Baseball Research's *Baseball Research Journal,* reveals the most frequent baseball nicknames since 1871. May we have the envelope?

1. Lefty
2. Red
3. Doc
4. Bud/Buddy
5. Dutch
6. Big (Jim, Bill, etc.)
7. Mickey
8. Whitey
9. Chick
10. Kid
11. Tex
12. Pop
13. Babe
14. Chief
15. Heinie
16. Pete
17. Fritz
18. Cy
19. Moose
20. Deacon

Others receiving votes: Rabbit, Rip, Blackie, Buster, Dixie, Butch, Sheriff, Happy, King, Pat, Jumbo, Pinky.

RED ALL OVER

It's a mere technicality that Lefty is, historically, baseball's most popular nickname. So there have been more lefthanders than redheads in the game. Red is still the consummate baseball nickname, time-tested and earthy as the game itself. Except for the occasional Donnie (Lefty) Moore (see p. 56), virtually every Lefty's been a southpaw; but not every Red's been a carrot-top. David Barron and Arthur Herring weren't, yet they were naturals for the nickname. Besides having had more than 100 players tabbed Red, baseball has two *teams* whose names feature the nickname, and the game has even been covered by some pretty good Reds (Smith, Barber) in their own right. As even the best steak can taste like a plain burger when doused in ketchup, Absalom Wingo lost his distinctive flavor when he was reduced to Red. But rather than seeing red over that unfortunate occurrence, let's examine the Reds who brought colorization to baseball long before Ted Turner bought the Braves:

Charles (Red) Adams
Leon (Red) Ames
Arnold (Red) Anderson
Morris (Red) Badgro
Donald (Red) Barbary
John (Red) Barkley
Emile (Red) Barnes
Charles (Red) Barrett
David (Red) Barron
James (Red) Bennett
James (Red) Bird
Henry (Red) Bittman
Harvey (Red) Bluhm
Edward (Red) Borom
James (Red) Bowser
Norman (Red) Branch
John (Red) Brown
Paul (Red) Busby
Howard (Red) Camp
Scott (Red) Cary
Cecil (Red) Causey
Allen (Red) Conkwright
John (Red) Connelly
Robert (Red) Daughters
Eugene (Red) Desautels
Francis (Red) Donahue
Charles (Red) Dooin
Alexander (Red) Downey
Jerome (Red) Downs
Elmer (Red) Durrett
Zebulon (Red) Eaton
Philip (Red) Ehret
Charles (Red) Embree
Russell (Red) Evans
Urban (Red) Faber

John (Red) Fisher
Thomas (Red) Fisher
Owen (Red) Friend
Woodward (Red) Gunkel
Ernest (Red) Gust
Myron (Red) Hayworth
Arthur (Red) Herring
Clifford (Red) Hill
Lloyd (Red) Hittle
Chester (Red) Hoff
Clarence (Red) Hoffman
James (Red) Holt
Murray (Red) Howell
Wilfred (Red) Johnston
Maurice (Red) Jones
John (Red) Juelich
Donald (Red) Kellett
Wade (Red) Killefer
Robert (Red) Kinsella
John (Red) Kleinow
Ralph (Red) Kreitz
Ralph (Red) Kress
Walter (Red) Kuhn
Kenneth (Red) Landenberger
Nelson (Red) Long
Charles (Red) Lucas
Louis (Red) Lutz
Japhet (Red) Lynn
John (Red) Marion
Frank (Red) McDermott
Ray (Red) McKee
Glenn (Red) McQuillen
Leo (Red) Miller
James (Red) Morgan
George (Red) Munger

Clarence (Red) Munson
John (Red) Murff
John (Red) Murray
Leo (Red) Nonnenkamp
John (Red) Oldham
Robert (Red) Ostergard
Thomas (Red) Owens
Ernest (Red) Padgett
Clarence (Red) Phillips
John (Red) Powell
John (Red) Rawlings
Charles (Red) Roberts
John (Red) Roche
Robert (Red) Rolfe
William (Red) Rollings
Charles (Red) Ruffing
Elbert (Red) Schillings
Albert (Red) Schoendienst

Maurice (Red) Shannon
Eugene (Red) Sheridan
Marvin (Red) Smith
Willard (Red) Smith
James (Red) Smyth
Thomas (Red) Stallcup
James (Red) Steiner
Robert (Red) Thomas
Walter (Red) Torphy
Stephen (Red) Tramback
Thadford (Red) Treadway
John (Red) Waller
Samuel (Red) Webb
Robert (Red) Wilson
Absalom (Red) Wingo
Al (Red) Worthington
Robert (Red) Worthington

Cliff (House) Levingston . . . because this NBA forward, his Atlanta Hawk teammates took delight in noting, hoisted up so many bricks that he could build one. A.k.a. Good News.

Rod (Rod Stupid) Gaspar . . . because, on the eve of the Orioles' 1969 World Series meeting with the Mets, Frank Robinson cried "Bring on Ron Gaspar!" When a teammate corrected him—"Not Ron, *Rod,* stupid"—Robinson said, "O.K., bring on Rod Stupid!"

Mike (Hercules) Weaver . . . because of his, well, Herculean build. Ken Norton started the nickname, which Weaver tried putting the kibosh on. "Hercules was a myth," he explained. "I'm not."

SATURDAY MORNING FEVER

With Saturday afternoon games following Friday nighters during much of the baseball season, it's difficult for a player to see his favorite animated shows on Saturday mornings. That hasn't kept cartoon characters from lending their names to ballplayers for use as nicknames. Here's our All-Cartoon Team:

Jerry (Popeye) Hairston. "Charlie Lau called me that. I hit a home run, and running around the bases I held my arms up a little. I guess that made me look like Popeye."

Steve (Sluggo) Garvey. Garv, too, has also been called Popeye, for his disproportionately large forearms.

Glenn (Yosemite Sam) Hubbard. At 5'8" and with that Grizzly Adams beard, he *is* the mountain man chasing that varmit Bugs Bunny.

Jim (Baby Huey) Maler. 6'4", 230 pounds.

Jim (Gumby) Gantner. Stormin' Gorman Thomas named him for the green-rubbery character. "For the way he walks," Thomas explained.

Tom (Wimpy) Paciorek. He subsisted solely on hamburgers while trying to support his family on a minor leaguer's salary. Dodger manager Tom Lasorda tagged him after the "I'll-gladly-pay-you-Tuesday-for-a-hamburger-today" character from the *Popeye* cartoons.

Milt (Fudd) May. As in Elmer. The two bear a haunting wesemblance to each other.

Fred (Flintstone) Gladding. When you look just like Bedrock's most famous resident *and* your first name is Fred, there's not much you can yabba-dabba do but accept this nickname gracefully.

Danny (Bam Bam) Walton. A teammate of Fred Gladding's in Houston in the early 1970s.

Reginald (Hooley) Smith . . . because this Hall of Famer's father thought he saw something of the Happy Hooligan cartoon character in his son.

The Smurfs . . . because this New York Rangers line of Mark Pavelich, Rob McClannahan and Anders Hedberg averaged 5'9½" and 175 pounds, and Philadelphia Flyer coach Bob McCammon likened them to the elfin creatures of Saturday morning cartoondom. The Washington Redskins followed by calling their diminutive receiving corps of Alvin Garrett and Virgil Seay the same thing.

HEAP BIG NAMES

Warren (Chief Running Mouth) Cromartie . . . because of this out-fielder's abundant gift of gab. When he fled Montreal for Japan, he marketed his own candy treat—the Cro-Bar—and so admired Yomiuri Giants slugger Saduharu Oh that he named his son Cody Oh Cromar-tie. Why not Oh Cro? Ran Cromartie's mouth: "I don't want my kid to remind people of a bottle of bourbon."

Chief Noc-A-Homeless . . . because Atlanta Braves mascot Chief Noc-A-Homa had his stadium teepee razed by owner Ted Turner to make way for more seats.

Robert (The Chief) Parish . . . because of this longtime Celtic center's ample size (7') and authoritative countenance. Or, perhaps, another reason. The apocryphal story is told of a blind radio reporter, trundled into the Celts' locker room after a game one night, extending his hand to a disrobed Parish by way of introduction. The journalist pressed unexpected flesh, and was heard to say, "Now I know why they call you The Chief."

BOOM BOOM AND HIS TEMPLE OF DOOM

In 1985, when Boris Becker was 1) first appearing on the tennis scene, 2) developing a pretty good serve, for a seventeen-year-old, and 3) winning Wimbledon with relative ease, writers scrambled to nickname the West German *Wunderkind*. "[His] red hair invites the nickname 'The Red Baron,' " quoth *The New York Times,* but as a nickname, The Red Baron didn't fly. To his screaming teenage fans, his peers, Becker became Boom Boom, an allusion to his alliterative real name and, more significantly, his cannonball serve.

Boom Boom's practice partner is another monster-server, a Yugoslav named Slobodan Zivojinovic (rhymes with nothing). Broadcasters prudently decided that he, too, needed a nickname, but he already had one: Bobo. While Boom Boom and Bobo serve BBs at each other in practice, their manager, a dark and droop-mustachioed Romanian named Ion (Dracula) Tiriac, looks on with megalomaniacal glee.

ALLITERATIVE APPELLATIONS

Tom (Terrific) Seaver . . . because "(New York *Daily News* scribe) Jack Lang wrote it. No one calls me that except the media."

Bob (The Vaulting Vicar) Richards . . . because this former pole vault star, who would later gain even more fame as a Wheaties pitchman, was an ordained reverend and avid Christian proselytizer.

C.C. (Cash & Carry) Pyle . . . because of his Barnumesque promotion of pseudo-sporting events in the 1920s and 1930s. A portent of the schlock *(refrigerator racing?)* to be served up on network television a half century later, Pyle's projects included the Bunion Derby of 1928, an eighty-four-day sprint from L. A. to New York. The footrace quickly became a fiasco, and had folks calling Pyle, whose given name was Charles, Corn & Callous.

(Wrong Way) Roy Reigels . . . because of that one play in the biggest game of his life, the 1929 Rose Bowl. California's Reigels scooped up a Georgia Tech fumble and took off for the goal line sixty yards away, despite 70,000 people screaming what would soon become his nickname. Teammate Benny Lom finally caught Reigels at his own three-yard-line and turned him around, but by that time Tech tacklers—it was hard to tell *who* was the Ramblin' Wreck here—had brought Reigels down at the one. A blocked punt then gave Tech a safety and an 8–7 win.

Archie (The Merry Mongoose) Moore . . . because this boxer said he had a "unique talent for ridding my life of snakes and rodents, some of which were people. I eliminated them from my path and mind. How? I got out of their way, simple as that."

Monsters of the Midway . . . because of the University of Chicago's Midway Plaisance the main drag on campus. The Midway's original Monsters were the U of C football teams coached by Amos Alonzo Stagg; when that school gave up fullback-bashing for atom-smashing, inept sportswriters transferred this inapt title to the city's dominant professional team, the Bears.

Red (The Galloping Ghost) Grange . . . because he could motor, he *was* an immortal and, well, sportswriter Grantland Rice had a thing for alliteration. (He gave us the Manassa Mauler, too.)

Jack (The Manassa Mauler) Dempsey . . . because he cut his teeth in Manassa, Colo., a town with a name tough enough to suit Dempsey who, in turn, put Manassa on the map. Still, we wonder: What if Jack had been weaned in neighboring Romeo, and been ring named accord ingly?

The Kamikaze Kids . . . because Dick Harter's Oregon Ducks of the early 1970s weren't quacks when it came to aggressiveness. The cover of their press guide featured a picture of every member of the starting five on the floor for a loose ball against UCLA.

The Bruise Brothers . . . because the San Antonio Spurs teams of early-1980s vintage featured such formidable bangers as Mark Olberding, Dave Corzine and Reggie Johnson up front.

Billy (The Kangaroo Kid) Cunningham . . . because, long before there were so many black players in the game, jumping was a skill that the white masses assumed only blacks had. This Brooklyn product had the hang of hang time.

The Embraceable Ewes . . . because what else are you gonna call the Los Angeles Rams' cheerleaders?

(The Bruise Brothers)

(Joltin') Joe DiMaggio . . . because, when you live a life that includes hitting safely in fifty-six consecutive games, taking Marilyn Monroe to the altar and having Simon and Garfunkel ask plaintively where you've gone, no other adjective quite fits.

(Dim) Dom Dallessandro . . . because he was short. Cubs announcer Bert Wilson first called this 5'6" outfielder Diminutive Dominic, then (appropriately enough) shortened the name to Dim Dom as a matter of convenience.

Canonero (The Caracas Cannonball) II . . . because this Derby long-shot winner was bred in Venezuela. In the Belmont, however, he bombed.

Richard (The Merchant of Menace) Burton . . . because this fellow, who was probably never married to Elizabeth Taylor, put the *bard* in bombardment.

Ted (The Splendid Splinter) Williams . . . because he was tall and thin, yeah, but because he swung a pretty splendid splinter of wood, too. As a name, though, the Splinter was hardly infectious. His teammates called him Kid, and Williams preferred Teddy Ballgame, the nickname he gave official sanction to in his autobiography.

Willie (The Bouncing Barrister) Banks . . . because this world-class triple-jumper holds a law degree.

DOUBLE FEETURE

Roll some footage from the early days in the life of Clarence (Foots) Walker. There he is sitting in his first-grade classroom, his size eleven shoes jutting from under his desk—and from under the desk in front of his. See the kids laughing at his big "foots"? Keep rolling . . . keep rolling . . . there! There's Foots in high school in Southampton, Long Island, filling some mighty big shoes on the basketball team—his own, of course, *and* those of Carl Yastrzemski, whose school scoring records are about to be broken. By Foots, to be exact. As Foots is starring for Cleveland and New Jersey in the NBA, let's stop the footage, dim the footlights and raise the curtain on our second feature.

These feet beneath the scorer's table belong to Nathaniel (Feets) Broudy, who ran the basketball clock at Madison Square Garden for three decades before retiring in 1986. Whence Feets? Again, we must rewind to his school days in Brooklyn, where neighborhood kids called him *Nisel,* an ordinary Yiddish nickname that became *Fisel,* the Yiddish word for feet. "My mother hated the name," he says. "Detested it." Why? Beats Feets, who has known no other name for most of his seventy-plus years. "Most people don't even know my real name," Nathan says. "They just know me as Feets."

Former Atlanta Braves publicist Bob (No, Not That One) Hope, on Cuckoo (Sea Cap) Christensen, a Cincinnati outfielder of the 1920s: "Why would anybody named Cuckoo need a nickname?"

NICKNAMES THOU SHALT NOT TAKE IN VAIN

Alonza (Allah the Rim God) Allen . . . because the man put the *slam* in Islam while at Southwest Louisiana.

Jeff (Monkey Jesus) Shepherd . . . because of some strange nickname breeding practices at the Madison Square Boys' Club in New York City, where Shepherd played before moving on to Kings River (Calif.) Community College. *Monkey* because his funny-looking shot lacked amazing grace; *Jesus* because it went in with amazing consistency. Monkey Jesus.

GOLDEN NOMERS

If nicknames spring from families, it follows that Notre Dame would spawn a passel of them. After all, the school in South Bend has college sports' largest extended family—from *echt* Golden Domers to the legions of Subway Alumni who have adopted the Irish as their own. Notre Damers have been known as the Fighting Irish since 1927, but were originally called the Catholics and—under the legendary Knute Rockne, who played an ambitious national schedule—the Ramblers.

George (The Gipper) Gipp, the infirm gridder immortalized by a certain President on the big screen and the man coach Rockne implored his team to win one for, is the *sine qua nom* of Notre Dame nicknames.

Superscribe Grantland Rice came up with The Four Horsemen after Harry Stuhldreher, Jim Crowley, Don Miller and Elmer Layden—mates in the Ramblers backfield—led the Domers to a 13–7 defeat of Army in 1924. Rice may have come up with the nickname on that steel gray October day, but he was too busy describing the color of the sky to figure out how to immortalize it. That was left to a student publicist named George Strickler, who posed the four footballers astride horses for a picture that transcends nicknames.

More recently, quarterback Joe Montana went through school nick-name-less, a situation one Bay Area newspaper tried remedying after he joined the NFL's San Francisco 49ers by holding a nickname-the-QB contest. The most inspired suggestion: Beaut.

But Notre Dame reserves her best nicknames for campus institutions who've never stepped on the field. Over the past 50 years, every under-grad has done his time in The Rock, the phys. ed. facility named for you-know-who. There, until his recent death, Edward (Fat Eddie) Kaz-mierzak kept order and dispensed towels.

Even the prez, the Rev. Edward (Monk) Molloy, comes tagged. (This erstwhile Irish hoopster called a childhood buddy Bunk, who in turn shot back with Monk. "It had nothing to do with piety or animallike behavior," says Molloy, who enters his own team—"All the President's Men"—in the campus's annual Bookstore Basketball Tournament.

Around campus, you'll spot the bronze statue outside Corby Hall, featuring the building's namesake with one arm aloft. He's Fair-Catch Corby. The Moses figurine, with one finger raised high, may be a not-so-subtle commandment to the wire-service pollsters. And that huge mural of Christ painted across the facade of Memorial Library—it lines up perfectly with the goal posts at the north end of the stadium—depicts Him with both arms upraised. He's Touchdown Jesus.

In the midst of all this, Irish basketball coach Richard (Digger) Phelps's nickname—because he's the son of an undertaker—doesn't sound quite sublime enough.

The Bad Bishops . . . because you need a tough name to run a certain kind of pawn shop in the Philadelphia ghetto. The Bad Bishops are an all-black championship chess team.

Larry (The High-Atolla of Slamola) Nance . . . because he won the first NBA Slam Dunk Contest. The Phoenix forward, who was also being called FlashNance, Mr. Slambassador and the Flying Sun, put a stop to the foolishness in his Edict of Nance, with which he declared he wanted nothing to do with such grandiose nicknames.

Goose (The Exorcist) Gossage . . . because "When he's out there on the mound," says Richie Zisk, "he scares the devil out of you." Goose,

Vaux Championship Chess Team (The Bad Bishops)

on the other hand, instills considerably less trepidation than his given Rich.

John (The Voice of God) Facenda . . . because this longtime narrator for NFL Films had a divine baritone that could lend drama to the most egregiously boring rout.

NAMES WITH PUNCH

Henry (Our 'Enery) Cooper . . . because of this heavyweight's immense popularity in his native Britain. The mute Cockney "H" also explains why his left hook was known as 'Enery's 'Ammer.

The Hammer of Thor . . . because Ingemar Johansson used this tool—his right hand—to make Swedish meatballs of most of his opponents. 'Enery's 'Ammer turned out to be of the ball-peen variety when confronted by The Hammer of Thor in a 1957 bout.

NOMINEES FOR BASEBALL'S OOKIE-OF-THE-YEARS

Nehames (Pookie) Bernstine
Harry (Cookie) Lavagetto
Willie (Mookie) Wilson

Lloyd (Little Poison) Waner . . . because Dodger fans razzed that Pirate for being a "little poison," which is Brooklynese for "little person." At 5'8", 150 pounds, Waner was certainly that. Brother/teammate/fellow Hall-of-Famer Paul Waner was Big Poison, despite being the same size as Lloyd, because he hit more homers and drove in more runs than Little Poison. (This explanation of the Waner brothers' nicknames may be apocryphal, but it's more interesting than the one always given by newsreel narrators of the 1930s: "Both are poison to opposing pitchers.")

Phil (Scooter) Rizzuto . . . because this Yankees shortstop's quick lateral movement enabled him to retrieve balls up the middle that second basemen couldn't reach. A grateful minor league teammate, Billy Hitchcock, nicknamed Rizzuto while watching the Scooter motor.

Edson Arantes (Pele) do Nascimento . . . because Brazilian sports stars have a habit of going by mononyms. There have been Socrates, Oscar and Tatu, too. But Pele was Brazil's—no, the world's—most celebrated athlete of the 1970s. "Edson is the normal person, he has defects," Pele has said. "One day he is going to be dead. But Pele, . . . he is never going to die. I have to deal with both, but I think the bigger responsibility is to Edson, because he was born first. I don't know why I became Pele. Only God knows."

Clarence (Bighouse) Gaines . . . because this 6'4", 300-pound plus coach at Winston-Salem State is an outsized small-college legend. There's no truth to the rumor that WSSU's Clarence Gaines Center is called The Bighouse.

THE CLYDES OF MARCH

After checking out *Bonnie and Clyde*, Walt Frazier bought himself the kind of wide-brimmed lid that Warren Beatty wore in the movie. The New York Knicks' secretary of dee-fense thus became a Clyde himself, from chapeau to toe, where his Puma sneaks bore the brand name *Clyde*.

Since Frazier, a new Clyde seems to pop up every other year. Those whose real names are Clyde, the rule goes, are nicknamed the Glide. Thus we've seen Clyde (The Glide) Bradshaw at DePaul and Clyde (The Glide) Drexler at Houston. And the first name shall be last: Florida State and, for one season, the Celtics, featured Benny (The Glide) Clyde and his bountiful Afro.

The last name of the newest cub in this pride of Clydes is Austin, and he played his college ball at North Carolina State. This Clyde the Glide was reportedly espied in a brand-new ride—as an undergrad—prompting Duke's Animals (the Blue Devils' notorious student section) to jingle car keys at Austin whenever he played in Durham.

SHADY CHARACTERS

Wayne (Tree) Rollins . . . because he's 7'1" and once sported a 'fro that provided shade for a family of four to picnic in. This is one Tree whose bark isn't as bad as his bite; the Finger Sandwich that Danny Ainge served him during the 1983 NBA Playoffs is now legend among Tree fans, who may or may not call themselves Druids.

Cliff (Old Treetop) Robinson . . . because Al McGuire forgot Robinson's name while telecasting one of Southern Cal's games, and repeatedly covered himself in the shade of this reference.

THE GANGS ARE ALL HERE

The somewhat addled world champion St. Louis Cardinals of 1934, The Gashouse Gang, were given their name *ex post facto* by Tom

Walt (Clyde) Frazier

Meany of the New York *World-Telegram*, or by Leo Durocher, or by reporter Frank Graham, depending on whom you believe. The main man of the 'house, of course, was Jay Hanna (Dizzy) Dean. Or Jerome Herman (Dizzy) Dean. The Diz not only gave reporters different names, but different birthdates, too, because he wanted each to have a scoop. Only the occasional Ruth, Berra or Julius Erving have had nicknames become as organic to a personality as Dean's Dizzy. Indeed, it's the only nickname to lend itself to science: a *mastophora dizzydeani* is a spider. In the words of Paul Harvey, "It's true."

Dizzy's brother Paul, on the other hand, may have been Daffy, but he wasn't daffy. He was a serious sort whose nickname was strictly for p.r. purposes. In fact, the team was as label-laden as any in history, carrying in addition to Dizzy and Daffy a Dazzy, Ducky, Lip, Tex, Wild Bill, Spud, Chick, Pepper and Ripper.* The Gang was managed by Frankie Frisch, The Fordham Flash, who replaced Charles (Gabby) Street for the start of 1934.

The Gashouse Gang's turf has extended to present-day baseball, as well. The Houston Astros have been called the Glasshouse Gang because of their home, the Astrodome, which in turn has been called The Dome on the Range. And the 1985 Cardinals won the National League pennant with a cast of exotics (see *Cuckoo Jar,* p. 57) that at least one scribe was moved to call The Nuthouse Gang.

RIVAL GANGS

Although Billy pitched for them for five seasons, the Cincinnati Reds of the mid-1960s were never known as McCool & the Gang. Let's celebrate, nonetheless, the Gangs that have flourished in sport:

The Dalton Gang. Pitchers Dick (The Turk) Farrell, Jim (The Bear) Owens and Jack (The Bird) Meyer raised hell *and* fines to unprecedented levels in 1960, but they couldn't raise the Phillies from last place.

The Gang of Four. When San Francisco defensive backs Ronnie Lott, Eric Wright, Carlton Williamson and Dwight Hicks came together in 1981, wall posters around the NFL announced other teams' receivers' demise.

The Gang of Six. Phillies phront-office phunctionaries Bill Giles, Tony Siegle, Jim Baumer, Paul Owens and Hugh Alexander, "plus whoever is managing," comprised the Gang of 1984, said one Phil. President Giles, who acted hastily in dispatching the Gang's business (releasing Pete Rose and firing beloved coach and former shortstop Bobby Wine on consecutive days), became Chairman Now.

The Over-the-Hill Gang. Led by Billy Kilmer (see *Hobble and Wob-*

---

*Vance, Medwick, Durocher, Carleton, Hallahan, Davis, Fullis, Martin and Collins, respectively.

ble, p. 120), these wrinkly-skinned Redskins beat the Cowboys for the 1972 NFC championship before losing to the unbeaten Dolphins in Super Bowl VII.

THEY'RE IN CHARGE

Rene (Captain Nemo) Lachemann . . . because he skippered the motley Brew Crew that rapidly sank to the American League East floor in 1984. Milwaukee Brewers, this was your Captain speaking: "I don't really like the nickname, but it's kind of funny, and so far it's true."

Bill (Captain Sominex) Belichek . . . because members of the Super Bowl XXI champion New York Giants defense, whom Belichek coordinated, were initially unmoved by his snoratory. Somehow, however, the message got through.

James (Captain Late) Silas . . . because this veteran ABA guard, a poised scorer and floor leader, always seemed to deliver down the stretches of games for the San Antonio Spurs.

ALIASES

Lester (The Molester) Conner . . . because of his many steals. Lester was sought and captured by two States—Oregon of the Pac-10 and Golden of the NBA—for frequently assaulting anyone who had a basketball indecently exposed.

Andrew (The Boston Strangler) Toney . . . because of the strain he put on Celtic windpipes in the 1982 Eastern Conference finals. By the time this 76er scorer released his choke hold in Game 7, it was too late for the Heimlich maneuver.

McFilthy and McNasty . . . because of the Bogart-like style of play Jeff Ruland and Rick Mahorn used when both were with the Washington Bullets. Scholars disagree as to which player was McFilthy and

James (Captain Late) Silas

which was McNasty, but are certain that the first to call them such was the Celtics' charitable announcer, Johnny Most. When Mahorn joined Detroit, Most called Mahorn and Piston teammate Bill Laimbeer McFilthy and McNasty. A discriminating fellow, that Johnny Most.

Ed (Strangler) Lewis . . . because this pro wrestler, who reigned during the 1920s when the sport was absolutely legit, had an inescapable headlock. Lewis won more than 6,200 matches—and lost but thirty-three times.

Daryle (The Mad Bomber) Lamonica . . . because, as an Oakland Raiders quarterback, he had a penchant for looking long to fleet receivers like Fred Biletnikoff and Warren Wells.

Marfa (The Mugger) . . . because this thoroughbred had a habit of violating the space of other horses in mid-race.

Jack (The Assassin) Tatum . . . because of his fierce play in the Raiders' defensive secondary. *They Call Me Assassin* is the title of his autobiography-confessional, and the nickname became horribly apt when Tatum paralyzed New England's Darryl Stingley with a hit in a preseason game.

Jeff (Penitentiary Face) Leonard . . . because, though Giants fans know he can do it all in Candlestick, he looks more like he did it *with* the candlestick, in the conservatory. Jeff did some time as both Hac-Man (a reference to his swing) and as *Sugar Ray* Leonard (after a fight with teammate Dan Gladden). Now that he insists on being called Jeffrey, his nickname has been adjusted accordingly. To Correctional Facility Face.

TYS THAT 'BOUND

With an average height of 5'3", this is basketball's All-Nickname, All-Time Small-Time Team, or our Not-So-High Five:

Tyrone (The Human Press) Bogues. Guard. A title he was given at Wake Forest, where he was indefatigable on defense for the Demon Deacons.

Tyrone (The Human Assist) Bogues. Guard. Doled out more dishes in his college career than a foreman in a Tupperware warehouse.

Tyrone (Muggsy) Bogues. Forward. Muggsy is a power forward's name, although Bogues first answered to it because Baltimore school-

Tyrone (Muggsy) Bogues

yard buddies thought his lightfingered backcourt style reminiscent of the *Bowery Boys* character.

Tyrone (La Chispa Negra) Bogues. Forward. *Small* forward, of course, but also quick. That's why fans at the World Basketball Championships in Madrid called him The Black Spark.

Tyrone (The PT Boat) Bogues. Center. A nickname straight from the hoarse mouth of Al McGuire, who calls big guys Aircraft Carriers.

Grandmaster Clash and the Furious Five . . . because, like music's Grandmaster Flash and the Furious Five, John Thompson and his 1984 NCAA Championship team were rap artists—rapping opponents with elbows, and talking abundant trash. Throughout that championship season, of course, Thompson made sure his players *didn't* rap with the press, which quickly labeled the atmosphere around the team Hoya Paranoia.

(Gentleman) Jim Corbett . . . because he once worked in a bank, and henceforth acted cordially and dressed spiffily. Indeed, in the ring he kept bankers' hours, shooing most of his opponents out early.

(Marvelous) Marv Throneberry . . . because someone scrawled that adjective above his locker nameplate during the Mets' marvel-less first season.

Charles (Good Night) Wright . . . because this slugger, a member of the legendary Steele's Sports softball team, averages two and a half home runs a game.

AND WE HASTEN TO ADD MIKE QUICK

If Nimble, Fast and Little didn't sound so much like a Lilliputian law firm, casual couch potatoes might assume that's what the letters NFL stand for. For more than a decade now, football has seen the development of a Speed Merchants Association that adheres to a no-returns policy: No kick returns, that is, unless you bear a nickname that connotes speed, dispatch or elusiveness. Witness:

Danny (Lightning) Buggs. Lightning caught touchdown strikes twice—and then some—as a wide receiver at West Virginia.

Sylvester (Postage) Stamps. Rarely takes a licking. This Atlanta Falcon returns to senders' end zones.

Eric (The Flea) Allen. Colts fans have seen him dog defenders, but rarely have they seen the Flea collared.

Noland (The Gnat) Smith. At 5'6¼", he was quite literally the lowest man on the Chiefs' totem pole, so he wore number 1. Gnaturally.

Renaldo (Skeets) Nehemiah. This world-class hurdler, who did a brief number as a 49er, might have lasted longer if Skeets had been short for Mosquito. Just ask The Flea and The Gnat.

Gerald (The Ice Cube) McNeal. Cleveland punter Jeff Gossett nicknamed McNeal when he noticed how slippery an ice cube was on a tabletop.

Eugene (Mercury) Morris. A peerless kick returner and occasional cocaine user as a Dolphin. After Mercury got high too often he spent time in the cooler.

LOCAL HEROES

Perry (The Manhattan Transfer) Bromwell . . . because this fast-footed guard left Manhattan College and enrolled at Penn, where at age twenty-four teammates called him Gramps.

Wilmer (Vinegar Bend) Mizell . . . because this erstwhile pitcher, who served ably in politics after his playing career ended, including as an assistant secretary of agriculture, hailed from a part of Alabama by that name.

TRAVEL ADVISORIES

An atlas worthy of Atlas might include these fighters:

Muhammad (The Louisville Lip) Ali
Lou (The Herkimer Hurricane) Ambers

Max (The Livermore Larruper) Baer
Paul (The Astoria Assassin) Berlenbach
Marcel (The Casablanca Clouter) Cerdan
Jim (The Roscommon Giant) Coffey
Billy (The Pittsburgh Kid) Conn
Johnny (The Chicago Spider) Coulon
Frank (The Harlem Coffee Cooler) Craig
Jack (The Manassa Mauler) Dempsey
Walter (The Kentucky Rosebud) Edgerton
Jim (The Kansas Rube) Ferns
Tiger (The Georgia Deacon) Flowers
Jim (The Pueblo Fireman) Flynn
Mike (The St. Paul Phantom) Gibbons
George (The Leiperville Shadow) Godfrey
Ace (The Nebraska Wildcat) Hudkins
Jack (The Galveston Giant) Johnson
Tommy (The Harlem Spider) Kelly
Stanley (The Michigan Assassin) Ketchel
Jake (The Bronx Bull) LaMotta
Sam (The Boston Tar Baby) Langford
Tippy (The Garfield Gunner) Larkin
George (The Saginaw Kid) Lavigne
Jock (The Rochdale Thunderbolt) McAvoy
Rocky (The Brockton Blockbuster) Marciano
Mike (The St. Paul Cyclone) O'Dowd
Billy (The Illinois Thunderbolt) Papke
Billy (The Fargo Express) Petrolle
Dwight (The Camden Buzzsaw) Qawi
Johnny (The Cleveland Rubber Man) Risko
Young (The Jersey Bobcat) Shugrue
Frank (The Sydney Cornstalk) Slavin
Jeff (The Bayonne Globetrotter) Smith
John L. (The Boston Strongboy) Sullivan
Joe (The Barbados Demon) Walcott
Ike (The Belfast Spider) Welk
Jess (The Pottawatomie Giant) Willard
Benny (The Tipton Slasher) Yanger

And, of course, Eligio Sardinias, who fought as Kid Chocolate—and inevitably became the Havana Bon Bon.

⚾ **Bert (The Minnesota Gopher) Blyleven** ... because this Twins pitcher served up a major league record of forty-nine home runs in 1986.

⚾ **Frank (The Pittsburgh Stealer) Tavares** . . . because this infielder stole more than 200 bases for the Pirates, including a league-leading seventy in 1977.

YOU'VE JUST BEEN HUSTLED BY RUDOLF WANDERONE, JR.

Like some poets and motel guests, billiards players cherish their anonymity, and with good reason, given some of the haunts and honchos associated with the game. Any pool player worth his chalk, then, will develop an alias. Broom-Handle Whitey's handle, for instance, is derived from his cue of choice, while Bruce the Horticulturist can really cultivate the green. Greasy Thumb Guzik has a slippery style, Inscrutable Joe and Deadpan Dan have faces of slate, while the rest of the pool hall roll call looks like a gazetteer. Boston Shorty. Philippine Gene. Jersey Red. And St. Louis Louie.

The man whose name is most synonymous with the anonymous world of pool sharks is Rudolf Wanderone, Jr. If Rudolf Sr. expected his son to carry on the family name, he'd be sorely disappointed. "I haven't heard my real name since I was three," says Rudolf, Jr., alias The Dean of Green, alias Triple Smart ("I was a genius as a kid," he explains). He was New York Fats in 1961, when *The Hustler,* a movie he boldly claims was based on his career, was made. Jackie Gleason's character went by *Minnesota Fats,* * however, and since then, Wanderone has too.

🏀 **Georgi (The Balkan Banger) Glouchkov** . . . because this bulky Bulgarian and ex-Phoenix Sun lacks finesse. Some Phoenicians weighed

---

*Minnesota Fats's geographic and physiognomic opposite is also familiar with tables upholstered in green felt: He's former World Series of Poker champion Amarillo Slim.

in with Air Georgi and Georgi Boy, but neither caught on. Glue didn't stick, either.

Thomas (Hollywood) Henderson . . . because this erstwhile Dallas Cowboys linebacker, whose star was on his helmet and not embedded in the Tinseltown sidewalk, was always in the spotlight. On the field he was ornery; off it, non-stop oratory. He *was* consistent; before Super Bowl XIII he predicted his 'Pokes would beat Pittsburgh 31–0. (The 'Wood got it half right; Dallas lost, 35–31.) Before the same game he also said, "Terry Bradshaw couldn't spell 'cat' if you spotted him the 'c' and the 'a'." (Bradshaw, the Steeler quarterback, was the game's MVP.) Soon thereafter, the Cowboys put Hollywood on permanent hiatus, and eventually, the law did much the same with various morals charges. He had one last fling, with the 49ers. After he missed three weeks of the 1980 exhibition season with minor injuries, his San Francisco mates dubbed him Holiday Henderson. (Curiously, it was *after* Henderson received his Hollywood nickname that he traveled to his nicknamesake and became a thespian of note, appearing in episodes of "Buck Rogers in the 25th Century" and "B. J. and the Bear," both on the small screen.) Has also been called The Mouth That Roared.

Dan (The Australian) Quisenberry . . . because of this relief pitcher's submarine, shoot-from-the-knee-delivery. Though the man who's also known as the Quiz was born in California, he comes from down under.

Rony (The Greek Peak) Seikaly . . . because this 6'10" center at Syracuse, though he grew up in Lebanon and is in fact an American citizen, is of Greek descent.

Eun Jung (Seoul Train) Lee . . . because she arrived from the Orient expressing her wish to bring a national championship to Northeast Louisiana. While that's hardly a loco motive for emigrating, might she have come if she'd known she'd also be called Chick Korea?

Georgi (The Balkan Banger) Glouchkov

Eun Jung (Seoul Train) Lee

OTHER THOUGHTS OF TRAINS

Walter (Big Train) Johnson . . . because he had the best fastball in the game at a time when the train was about the fastest thing on earth.

Lionel (Little Train) James . . . because *all* guys named Lionel are nicknamed Train. The modifier was thrown in because this Auburn and NFL scatback is only 5′6″.

Dick (Night Train) Lane . . . because a Lions teammate named Ben Sheets noticed how much this Hall of Fame defensive back liked band-leader Buddy Morrow's rendition of "Night Train."

Pittsburgh Steelers guard Sam (Rock) Davis, elaborating on a club questionnaire as to how he acquired his nickname: "Because of my solid hitting ability."

NOMS DE PLUMAGE

Tris (The Gray Eagle) Speaker . . . because he circled center field with grace and without Grecian Formula. Teammates spake of Speaker as *Spoke.*

George (The Stork) Theodore . . . because the 6′5″, 190-pound former Met was given the nickname *all* gangly guys eventually get. Unlike most storks, however, this lifetime .219 hitter didn't deliver.

Y. A. (The Bald Eagle) Tittle . . . because when he'd take to the field and strap his helmet on he had no heir apparent; when he took it off, he still had no hair apparent.

Tom (The Flamingo) Brennan . . . because of the unorthodox manner in which he delivers. The Dodger reliever kicks his left knee waist-high and holds it there, while perched on one leg, before whipping his right arm around with the pitch.

Ted (The Mad Stork) Hendricks . . . because he seemed to have something loose upstairs, and because upstairs was 6'8" off the ground. At one training camp, Raider coaches found The Stork relaxing beneath an umbrella while two women fanned him and fed him grapes; meanwhile, his teammates were running their prescribed laps around him. Sounds perfectly sane to us.

Mark (The Bird) Fidrych . . . because the Muppet-like mop and awkward gangliness of this pitcher resembled "Sesame Street's" Big Bird. Mark was also indirectly responsible for the nickname of another major league pitcher, Doug (The Fidrych) Bird.

Reece (Goose) Tatum . . . because this remarkable athlete, who played a couple of years of Negro League baseball before embarking on a legendary career with the Harlem Globetrotters and Magicians, had an 84" arm span and enormous hands.

Phil (The Vulture) Regan . . . because this reliever allowed the pitchers preceding him to ravage the opposition before he deigned to swoop in, feast on the carrion and flap off with a save.

DUCK SOUP

It couldn't happen today because women don't talk like that anymore. When Joe (Ducky) Medwick took his post in the Cardinals' outfield and teammates overheard a lady in the stands squeal, "He's so ducky-wucky," St. Louis had a Ducky to add to its Dizzy and Daffy. (Today, the liberated female fan speaks as good —or bad a game as the male, and is apt to be yelling something not fowl but foul.)

Dick (Ducky) Schofield played shortstop for the Cards in the 1950s. Was the same woman ogling ballplayers for two decades? Will Ozzie Smith be renicknamed Ducky Smith by a Busch Stadium nonagenar-

Tom (The Flamingo) Brennan

ian? Whatever, zoologists are baffled that Schofield's son Dicky, a California Angel, did not become a Duckling.

It's open season not only on Cardinals but on Donalds, all of whom receive Duck billing some time in their lives. Notre Dame shooting guard Donald (Duck) Williams knew this. When the Irish were scheduled to play in Christmas tourneys, they didn't want Cold Duck for the holidays.

Fairleigh Dickinson hooping bird Redonia (Red) Duck survived a nasty car crash, and thanked his ducky stars that his nickname didn't become Dead. Korean boxer Duk Koo Kim wasn't so fortunate, dying from blows to the head received in a bout with Ray (Boom Boom) Mancini.

And Erskine (Duck) Wade is the only fighter whose nickname consisted of advice to his opponents.

Billy (Daffy Duck) Sample . . . because, this former major leaguer says, "I'm black, I've got big feet and I'm always bitching."

AND A DUCK OF A DIFFERENT FEATHER . . .

Sloan (Duck Butter) Price . . . because that's what this stable groom should have done when someone threw a dish of Grade A at him during a dispute in a track kitchen. Price didn't, and received a scar and a nickname he would carry through his long career.

THEY'RE JAMMIN' WITH A JAILHOUSE ROCK

For too many coulda-been basketball stars who can't confine their shooting to the courts (or are confined by a court for their shooting), dreams of seeing playing time before a full house give way to the reality of *doing* time in the big house. Still, a few of the folks who put the "J" in jail find fame inside its walls, earning aliases that say it all.

Kind John played his ball at Attica, where his sterling jump shot and a heart of gold combined to form an amiable enough alloy: Playing a yard game of one-on-one for cigarettes one day, he got his honorific when he *didn't* off a fellow inmate he'd whipped who wouldn't fork over the smokes.

The Milkman's route took him through Petersburg, Va., where he honed his hooping skills against the likes of Moses Malone. He was sentenced to prison and given his nickname for precisely the same reason. As Mo tells us, it's " 'cause he murdered a milkman, man."

Tony (T) also played his ball in the Commonwealth. This high school stud heard P.A. announcers cry countless times a game, "T for two!" Alas, Tony went up on assault charges before his career fully blossomed, and those folks in Virginia who remember him at all now know him as "T for two-to-ten."

Lorne (Gump) Worsley . . . because you'd settle on Gump, too, if you had to deal with "Lorne Worsley." (Try saying it three times fast.) Seriously, this former New York Ranger, who found himself in a bitter contract dispute with that team, might just as well have been called Grump. Asked upon retiring what club had given him the most trouble, he replied, "The New York Rangers."

(Shoeless) Joe Jackson . . . because he first played baseball barefoot in the park. When Shoeless finally did don footwear, the hose he chose became soiled. As a member of the Black Sox, the 1919 White Sox who conspired to throw the World Series and thus were renamed, Jackson moved one young fan to cry the immortal, "Say it ain't so, Joe!"

Ewell (The Whip) Blackwell . . . because he was tall (6'6") and extremely thin and delivered his pitches sidearm, as if cracking a whip. Shame on those who thought the nickname was of disreputable origin.

SIGNS OF A TIME

A generation of ballplayers, each with a CPA's first name and B-movie star's nickname, came to the fore in the 1950s—folks like Eldon (Rip) Repulski, Everett (Rocky) Bridges and Forrest V. (Spook) Jacobs.

Baseball cards always identified such creatures by their nicknames, even if the players themselves seemed to prefer gracing the cards with facsimile signatures of their impossibly stodgy given names. Thus, Coot Veal affixed "Orville Veal" to his card, and Cot Deal signed his "Ellis F. Deal."

These gentlemen sorely needed the nicknames they got. Too bad they wouldn't put 'em on the line.

William (Dummy) Hoy . . . because, as a deaf-mute, he couldn't hear an umpire bellow "Ball" or "Stee-rike." To fill Hoy in on the count, legend has it, umps graciously raised a right hand when calling a strike. And they've been doing it ever since.

Andre (Pulpwood) Smith . . . because this former Georgia running back's father owned a lumber mill. His brothers are nicknamed Chainsaw and Sawdust.

Lloyd (Shaker Mo) Moseby . . . because of this slugger's ability to shake and bake on the basketball court. The nickname, which graces his bats and glove, is dear to Moseby. "We're the best," he once said of the Blue Jays in spring training. "Take it from Shaker."

THE GREAT AMERICAN PASTIME, WITH SUBTITLES

It takes a Berlitz course in baseball nicknames to know that foreign players are tagged: a) in their native tongues, b) in English, or c) in a curious hybrid of both of the above.

Tony (El Gato) Pena was nicked in the Dominican Republic for his stealthy, cat-quick moves in foiling would-be base stealers. Japanese pitcher Ytaku Enatsu answers to *ippiki okami,* which sounds like it would taste great over noodles, but translates to Lone Wolf. Indeed, Enatsu was one of very few Nipponese players—if not the *ippiki* one— to flee the Orient for America, where he had an unsuccessful tryout with Milwaukee.

The Spanish-to-English half of the nickname dictionary includes

Fernando (Tortilla Fats) Valenzuela, who was born and fed in Mexico; and Roberto Clemente of the Dominican Republic, who was The Great One in Pittsburgh and his homeland. And for the bilingual "coup de gracie," to borrow one of Bugs Bunny's multilingual malaprops, there's Aurelio Lopez, who speaks Spanish and pitches with plenty of English. He's called Señor Smoke.

Gary (Ding-Dong) Bell . . . because of the sound made when one of this pitcher's frequent deliveries in the dirt struck his catcher in the protective cup. We can thank Jim Bouton, Bell's former Seattle Pilots teammate and author of the confessional *Ball Four,* for enlightening us about this nickname and its raunchy derivation.

Bob (Foothills) Kurland . . . because that was the relative elevation from which Oklahoma A&M opponents hoisted shots against this mountainous seven-footer. He and George Mikan lorded over college hoops in the mid-1940s so absolutely that they mothered the goaltending rule.

(Wahoo) Sam Crawford . . . because he came up on the banks of the majestic Wahoo Creek, in Wahoo, Nebraska. Yippee!

AND THEN THERE'S THE WRIGHT BUBBAS, AND THE BUBBAS KARAMAZOV . . .

Bubba serves dubba duty as a nickname. It's given to the eldest son in some Southern families, and to the youngest son in others. When a babbling toddler mispronounces "Brother" as "Bubba," the bro' being addressed often keeps the handle. Other times, "Bubba" sticks to the baby.

The popular notion that Bubba is a nickname reserved for fat black kids simply isn't true. In fact, many whites have been dubbed Bub, too. Bubba Jennings, a former Texas Tech hoopster, is of the Caucasian persuasion (though clearly most basketball players named Bubba are *not*), as is Emery (Bubba) Church, who prospered for the Phils in the

1950s. Could he have done otherwise in the City of Bubba-ly Love?

The other myth about Bubbas is that they're all behemoths. They're not, notwithstanding the biggest and best-known of them, ex-footballer Bubba Smith, who's no lightweight despite his favorite brand of beer. Ain't he heavy? He's a Bubba.

Ronald (Goings) Anderson . . . because this NHL forward, in light of his having played with four different minor and four more major league clubs, could only be called this. Or Comings.

Orville (Sarge) Moody . . . because, before charging onto the PGA Tour, he spent fourteen years in the Army, winning the 1965 All-Service Championship and three Korean Opens.

NICKNAMES NON GRATA

It's tough to become a truly feared force in the City Game when folks know you as Zeke from Cabin Creek, or The Hick from French Lick. That's precisely why Jerry West and Larry Bird found their nicknames nothing to write home to West Virginia and Indiana about. West was fortunate, burying his nickname as readily as he did twenty-foot jumpers at the horn. Mr. Clutch became his new title, and the title of his autobiography. Bird, too, shed his tag: The Hick from French Lick doesn't fit on the MVP trophy.

Jockey William (Willie) Shoemaker wanted to shoo away his two nicknames, quite naturally preferring the diminutive Bill to either Willie or Shoe. The Phils' and White Sox' Richard/Richie (Call Me Dick) Allen campaigned for his nickname. Wilting at the Stilt, Wilt Chamberlain also had a preference for a different form of deference. He loved to be called The Big Dipper, and still calls his home, filled with Dipper-sized furnishings, Ursa Major.

Which brings us to the curious case of Charles (Lefty) Driesell. Or is it Lefty (Charles) Driesell? He has no hairdresser, much less hair, so nobody knows for sure. Driesell had been called Lefty since his school days in Norfolk, Va., but in 1985 he decreed to the media that he was no longer to be referred to by his nickname. "Being called Lefty is disrespectful," he said. "I'm fifty-three and I don't like to be called by a nickname." Shortly thereafter, he said he merely wanted every *Lefty* in the Terrapins' press guide changed to *Charles G.* "I just prefer it that way," he said, adding, "The whole thing has been blown way out of proportion."

Finally, Driesell allowed, "I still sign autographs Lefty." Was he granting permission to refer to His Southpawedness again? "You can call me Lefty," he said. "Call me whatever you want—as long as you call me." Less than a year later, Maryland called for his resignation.

Frank (Raffles) Boucher . . . because this honorable gentleman from hockey's early days spent a year raising the fifty dollars he needed to buy his release from the Mounted Police, which he'd joined as a seventeen-year-old. Once making it into pro hockey, he won the Lady Byng Trophy for sportsmanship seven times.

Mitch (The Bitch) Richmond . . . because this Kansas State player was a wild 'Cat, tough to handle at both ends of the floor.

Von (Old 5-4-1) Hayes . . . because of a trade, *not* because of any tendency to hit into third-to-second-to-pitcher double plays. The Phils sent Manny Trillo, Julio Franco, George Vukovich, Gerry (Rats) Willard and Jay Baller to Cleveland in exchange for Hayes.

James (Quick) Tillis . . . because this Chicago heavyweight didn't dally on the draw. He did lose to Carl (The Truth) Williams, however, proving once again that the Truth will out.

BAR GAME #4/MATCHED PAIRS

(Mean) Joe Gergen of *Newsday* and former Philadelphia *Daily News* columnist John (Superbrat) Schulian play a game whose lone rule is this: apply nicknames of athletes to people in other fields who share that athlete's first or last name. The object is to make the nickname as appropriate as possible. Schulian, for 'instance, lent boxer Carl (The Truth) Williams's handle to disgraced former New Jersey Senator Harrison (The Truth) Williams. Gergen reserved it for the gal who was stripped of her Miss America crown when she didn't disclose that she'd posed nude for photos that later appeared in *Penthouse:* Vanessa (The Truth) Williams.

Members of Gergen's Hall of Fame include Elizabeth (Fatty) Taylor, Tina (Bulldog) Turner and Leo (The Lip) Tolstoy. Schulian weighs in with Helen Gurley (Three Fingers) Brown.

As a warmup to your own game, we challenge you with a basketball team composed of ex-commanders-in-chief. They are: No. 1, George (Pearl) Washington; No. 35, John (Choo) Kennedy; No. 7, Andrew (Action) Jackson; No. 36, Lyndon (Magic) Johnson; and No. 4, James (Master Blaster) Madison. Since this is an all-presidents game, we'll play it in Philadelphia, where the presidency was created—and follow Gergen's suggestion to have a Philly fixture sing *God Bless America* before the game. That's right: Kate (Bonecrusher) Smith.

Jack Buck, while working with George (Sparky) Anderson on the radio broadcast of the 1986 World Series, brought up the curious first name of Spike Owen, the Boston Red Sox shortstop.

> Buck: " 'Spike' isn't Owen's nickname. It comes from 'Spikes,' which was his mother's name."
> Sparky: "What was her last name?"

Harry (Punch) Broadbent . . . because this iceman of the 1920s, a frequent visitor to the penalty box, had, in his words, "a hard time controlling my elbows." His fists, evidently, too.

Demetreus (Me) Gore . . . because it's short for Demetreus, he'll tell you. Then again, so is Us. The truth is, as an underclassman at Pitt, he had a penchant for selfish, one-on-one play.

Steve (Rainbow) Trout . . . because, in nicknaming him, his teammates chose an angling angle—though Rainbow could have just as easily assumed his father's nickname. After all, Paul (Dizzy) Trout passed on a touch of vertigo to his son, who missed part of the 1985 season with the Cubs after falling off a bicycle. A *stationary* bicycle.

Darrell (MX) Green . . . because the winner of "The Fastest Man in the NFL" competition has speed and—Redskin opponents will tell you—first-strike capability. (This is the kind of nickname they tend to give in Washington.)

'VILLE 'N' 'NOVA: WILD CATS

In 1985, Villanova cut its starting five and went on to win the national championship. The next year, Louisville won it all after getting rid of *its* first five. College basketball teams, it seems, do just fine without the first five letters in their schools' names, as champs 'Nova and the 'Ville can attest.

Letters, in fact, have become almost as important as players nowadays. You gotta know which ones to axe, which to keep and all along strive for *chemistry*. The 'Ville and 'Nova kept the right syllables and beat teams that couldn't match up at the nickname position. Villanova beat Georgetown in the finals: George? How about the 'Town? Louisville had an even easier time in the 1986 championship games. The 'Ville played monosyllabic Duke, a school whose name doesn't lend itself easily to truncation: Du? The 'Uke? *Great seats, eh buddy?*

As institutions for higher nicknaming go, the 'Ville is clearly the Coupe de. The 1980 Cardinals (that's their mundane, *official* nickname) dubbed themselves the Doctors of Dunk, and Darrell (Dr. Dunkenstein) Griffith designed their warmup tops to look "just like doctors' smocks." Among Dunkenstein's (a.k.a. Louisville's Living Legend) scrub nurses were Carlton (Scooter) McCray—he was his mother's "little Scooter Pie"—and one (Never Wrong) Poncho Wright, who signed his name that way. Derek Smith and Wiley (Coyote) Brown declared at the start of the season, "The 'Ville is going to the 'Nap." Sho' 'nuff, the 'Ville was cutting down the nets in Indianapolis six months later.

The 'Ville was king of the hill in 1986 with just as many nicknames.

They had a cool guard, Milt (Ice) Wagner (so named, he said, "because of my 'ice-o-lation' move"), and an icier freshman center, (Never Nervous) Pervis Ellison, whose name would grace both the MVP trophy and "Soul Train's" Word Scramble. Herb Crook was Superb, in nickname at least, and Billy Thompson was World, an a.k.a. he got as a freshman from skeptical upperclassmen unimpressed by his showboating.

A regular bridesmaid in the Final Four, Memphis State is runner-up in the name game, too. Tiger players of mid-1980s vintage called one another by monosyllables whenever they wanted to sound clannish. Thus Vincent Askew was 'Skew, William Bedford was Bed and Baskerville Holmes, as if he needed a nickname, became Bat. Andre Turner, who was labeled Andre Turnover when he was more cavalier with the basketball and who became the Little General when he finally snapped to attention, was merely 'Dre to 'mates Bed, Bat and 'Skew.

Bob (Mute Rockne) Pulford . . . because of this Chicago Black Hawks coach's laconic style of leadership.

Louis (Matchsticks) Orr . . . because he's 6'9" and weighs only 190 pounds. He was billed as a co-star in "The Louie and Bouie Show" at Syracuse, in which 'Sticks shared credit with 6'10" Roosevelt (speaks softly but looks like a Big Stick) Bouie. A.k.a. Gandhi.

(Starvin') Marvin Freeman . . . because this Phils pitcher has no curve: he's 6'7" and weighs only 182 pounds. Also known as Manute Base-Bol.

SOMEONE THIS BIG
DESERVES MORE THAN ONE NICKNAME

Manute ('Nute Blockne) Bol . . . because of this 7'6" center's knack for the blocked shot. And because he can give unequalled halftime speeches, unless someone else speaks Dinka dialect.

Manute (The Human Pencil in Sneakers) Bol . . . because this 7'6" Dinka dunker first reported to the Washington Bullets weighing 190 pounds.

 Manute (Rudy) Bol . . . because Bullets teammate Jeff Malone decided his Sudanese teammate needed to be Americanized, and this nickname would be a good start.

SOMEONE *MISTAKEN* FOR SOMEONE THIS BIG DESERVES MORE THAN ONE NICKNAME, TOO

Kevin (Manute Bol) McHale . . . because someone mistook this 6'11" Irish-American for the 7'6" Sudanese tribesman at Washington National Airport. "You're *not* Manute Bol?" inquired the skeptical fan. "No," McHale replied. "Not the last time I looked in the mirror."

Kevin (The Black Hole) McHale . . . because "When you throw the ball into him," says Celtics teammate Danny Ainge, "it never comes out."

YOU TELL US

Some baseball nicknames defy explanation. Jim (Abba Dabba) Tobin must have done *something* to warrant his tag; the Flintstonian question is, "What did Abba Dabba do?" Wedunno. Nor do we know whence these came:

Jimmy (Foxy Grandpa) Bannon
Horace (Dooley) Womack
Francis (Bots) Nekola
Hugh (Ee-Yah) Jennings
Charles (The Old Woman in the Red Cap) Pabor

Kevin (The Black Hole) McHale

WE DON'T WANNA KNOW

Frank (Booger) Welch
George (Hickie) Wilson
Wayne (Footsie) Belardi
Alfred (Greasy) Neale
Harry (Stinky) Davis

(WE ALMOST FORGOT)

Lawrence (Yogi) Berra . . . because when he was a squat fifteen-year-old, his friends in St. Louis thought he resembled the squatting yogi they had seen in a movie. Until that point Yogi had been called Lawdy by his family. Now, of course, "Everybody calls me Yogi. If I walked down the street and somebody yelled, 'Hey, Larry,' I know I wouldn't turn around."

Lawrence (Yogi) Berra

Index

NICKNAMES

A-Train, the, 42
Abba Dabba, 174
Abominable No-Man, the, x
Ace from Space, the, 56
Ach, 87
Ack Ack, 134
Action, 171
Actual Retail, 3
Ain'ts, the, 74
Aircraft Carrier, 155
Air Georgi, 149
Airhead, 57
Albino Rhino, the, 26
Allstate, 94
Almost, 94
Along Came, 4
Alphabet Man, the, 42
Amana, 72
Amarillo Slim, 158
-American, 5
American Tourister, 104
America's Team, 67
Amityville Horror, the, 106
Ancient Mariner, the, 75
and, 6
Andre Turnover, 173
Animal, the, 85
Anne Murray offense, 29
Antelope, the, 75
Antman, the, 29
Apathy, 97
Arnie's Army, ix, 32
Assassin, the, 15, 153
Astoria Assassin, the, 157
Astronaut, the, 11
Atom Bomb, 134
Australian, the, 159
Autobiography of Miss Jane, the, 6
Autrichienne, l', x
Avalanche, 117

Babe, 135
Babe, the, 20, 22
Babe Ruth's Legs, 22
Baby Beef, 24
Baby Huey, 138

Bad News, 47
Badger, the, 11
Bald Eagle, the, 162
Balkan Banger, the, 158
Bambam, 138
Bambino, 20, 41
Bananas, xii
Band-Aid, 30
Bar, 5
Barbados Demon, the, 157
Barber, the, 50–1
Barney Rubble Face, 125
Baron, 37
Basque Wood Chopper, the, 111
Bat, 173
Batman, 78
Battling Barkeep, the, 130
Bayonne Globetrotter, the, 157
Beano, 31
Bear, 1, 60
Bear, the, 150
Beaver, the, 23
Bed, 173
Bedtime Story, a, 6
Beetle, 6
Be Home, 3
Belfast Spider, the, 157
Ben, 15
Bernie and Ernie Show, the, 120
Big, 135
Big Daddy, 125
Big Daddy Dawg, 64
Big Dipper, the, 169
Big E., the, 42, 98
Big Game, 101
Bighouse, 147
Big John Studd, 101
Big O, the, 42
Big Poison, 147
Big Red, 14
Big Six, 40
Big Train, 162
Billy, 36
Bird, x

Bird, the, 150, 163
Bird Thou Never, 87
Biscuit, 117
Bitch, the, 170
Black Betsy, 20, 27
Blackenroe, 101
Blackie, 120, 135
Black Hole, the, 174
Black Magic, 99
Black Moses, 76
Black Rambo, 109
Black Shadow of Leiperville, the, 84–5
Black Spark, 155
Black Uhlan of the Rhine, 85
Blame It on, 3
Blind Bomber, the, 113
Blue Moon, 59
Blue Notes and the, 4
Bob & Carol & Ted & Dallas, 126
Bobo, 140
Bo Derek, the, 45
Bone, the, 51
Bonecrusher, 85, 171
Boo, 104, 125
Boobie, 2, 125
Boo Boo, 9, 104, 125
Booger, 176
Boom Boom, 89, 139–40, 165
Boomer, 83
Boris Boogie, ix, 69
Born in the U.S., 4
Boss, 58
Boss, the, x
Boston Baked Bean, the, 31
Boston Shorty, 158
Boston Strangler, the, 81, 151
Boston Strongboy, the, 157
Boston Tarbaby, the 157
Bots, 174
Bouncing Barrister, the, 143
Bow Wow, 87
Boy, xii
Boy Gorge, 72
Bozo, 9

Brandy, 5
Bread Truck, 72
Brew, 104
Brillo, 94
Broadway, 2
Broderick Crawford Highway Patrol, the, 109
Bronx Bombers, the, 20
Bronx Bull, the, 157
Broom-Handle, 158
Brother Low, 97
Brothers, 4
Brown Bomber, the, 8
Brown's Bombers, the, 8
Bruise Brothers, 141
Bubba, ix, 108–9
Buckshot, 115
Buc Stoppers, the, 63
Bud, 135
Buddy, 135
Buffalo, 6
Buffy, 44
Bull, 75
Bulldog, 171
Bum, 1
Bum, the, xii
Bump City, 85
Bunny, the, 27
Bunny, 88
Business Partner, 27
Buster, 135
Butch, 135
Buzzsaw, 113

Cadillac, 93
Cakes, 17
Cal, 121
California Quake, the, 69
Camden Buzzsaw, the, 157
Captain Late, 151
Captain Nemo, 151
Captain Outrageous, 65
Captain Sominex, 151
Caracas Cannonball, the, 142
Car Please, the, 6
Casablanca Clouter, the, 157
Casey, 115
Cash & Carry, 140
Cat, the, 23, 85
Catfish, 60
Catman, 64
Caveman, 12
Chainsaw, 167
Chairman Now, 150
Chairman of the Board, the, x
Chairman of the Boards, the, 44
Champ, 85
Channel, 66
Charles Dickens, 37
Cheese, xiii, 88
Chewbacca, 40
Chi Chi, 122
Chicago Spider, the, 157
Chick, 135, 150

Chicken on the Hill Will, 17
Chief, the, 139
Chief Noc-A-Homeless, 139
Chief Running Mouth, 139
Chili, 39–40
Chispa Negra, la, 155
Chocolate Thunder, 89
Choo, 104, 125, 171
Choo Choo, 104
Chris, 50
Church, 6
Clams, 4
Claude Rains, 107
Claw, the, 78
Cleveland Rubber Man, the, 157
Clyde, 148
C'mon People Now, 4
CNN, 94
Coach K, 42
Coach V, 42, 43
Cobra, the, 24
Coke-Is-It, 12
Colada, 5
Cookie, 147
Cool, 58
Cooled Heat, 45
Cool Papa, 58
Coot, 167
Corn & Callous, 140
Cornbread, 19
Cosmetics Kid, the, 105
Cot, 167
Cotton, 4
Count, x
Count, the, 10
Coyote, 172
Crackle, 130
Crambo, 109
Cranberry, 5
Crazy Horse, 57
Crazy Legs, ix
Crocodil, le, 23
Crocodile, 4
Crunch Berries, the, 28
Crystal, 87
Cuckoo Jar, 57, 150
Curly, 38, 109
Cutty Sark, the, 45
Cy, 126, 135
Cy Clone, 126

Daddy Bags, 61
Daffy, 150, 163
Daffy Duck, 165
Dah, 5
Daiquiri, 5
Dalton Gang, the, 150
Damien, 81
Danimal, 64
Dawgs, the, 63–4
Dazzy, 150
/DC, 4
Deacon, 135
Dead Fish, the, 45
Dean of Green, the, 158

Death to Flying Things, 14–5
Defroster, the, 118
Der Bingle, x
Diaper Squad, the, 75
Dick Vitalis, 39
Diesel, the, 125
Dig 'Ems, 56
Digger, 145
Dim, 142
Ding Dong, 168
Dinnerbell, x
Dipper, the, 17, 126
Dipstick, 132
Ditto, 34, 36
Dixie, 68, 135
Dizzy, 149–50, 163, 172
D.J., 81
Doc, 1, 20, 76, 78, 80, 105, 135
Doc Nice, 76
Doctor, the, 78
Dr. Death, 76
Dr. Doom, 76
Dr. Du, 78
Doctor Dunkenstein, 78, 172
Dr. J., 43, 76, 98
Dr. K., 76
Doctors of Dunk, the, 78
Dr. Strangeglove, 81
Dog, 23
Doggie, 22
Dollar, 124
Dome on the Range, ix
Donna, 25
Don't Call Me Charlie, 60
Don't Wear Plaid, 5
Dooley, 174
Doomsday Defense, the, 63
Doran, 4
Double O, 14
Downtown, 104
Dracula, 140
Drama in Bahama, ix, 38
Driftwood, 28
Dristan, 72
Drummer Boy, the, 1
Duck, 165
Duck Butter, 165
Ducky, 150, 163
Duke, x
Dummy, 167
Dusty, 87
Dutch, 132, 135

Earl, the, 128
Eat-'Em Up, xi
Ebony Eyes, 4
Eclipse, 127
Ecological Fastball, the, 45
Eephus Pitch, the, 45
Ee-yah, 174
Eggs, 5
Elephant Drawers, the, 31
Elevator Man, the, 52
Elmer, 9
Emergency, 36

End Zone, 115
Endorser, the, 117
Ernie D., 22, 43
Ernie No D., 22
ESPNosa, 3
E.T., 106
Ethel, 4
Evil Doctor Blackheart, 81
Exorcist, the, 145
Exterminator, the, 51
Eyechart, 87
Eyes, 4

Fair-Catch Cosby, 145
Fargo Express, the, 111, 157
Fat, xii, 61, 72
Fat Albert, 55
Fat Butt, 128
Fat Daddy, 91
Fat Eddie, 145
Father Time, 58
Fatty, 78, 171
Fayette, 72
Fearsome Foursome, the, 61
Feets, 143
Fernando's Fadeaway, 45
Fettuccini, 3
Fiddlin' Five, 37
Fidrych, the, 163
Fifi, 40
Fifth Avenue, 8
Fighting Irish, the, 144
Fire, 88
Fireball, 106
First Mama, x
Fishin' Magician, 52
Fist, the, 85
Flamingo, the, 163
FlashNance, 145
Flea, the, 156
Flick, 122
Flinstone, 138
Flip, 50
Floating, 7
Fly, 25
Flying Sun, the, 145
Foggy, 127
Fonz, the, 133
Food World, 72
Foothills, 168
Foots, 143
Footsie, 176
Fordham Flash, the, 150
Fort Landry, 9
46 Defense, the, 124
Four Horsemen, the, 144
Four Tops, the, 129
Foxy Grandpa, 174
Fran the Man, 87
Frank Sinatra, the, 45
Freddy, 108
Free, 3
French Connection, the, 110
Frenchy, 15, 134
Freud, 37
Fritz, 135

Frosty, 127
F-Troop, the, 69
Fudd, 138
Full Pack, 57
Furniture, 87
Fuzzy, 97

Gabby, 150
Gag Line, the, 110
Gallo, 66
Galloping Ghost, the, xii, 141
Galveston Giant, the, 157
Gang of Four, the, 150
Gang of Six, the, 150
Garfield Gunner, the, 157
Garrulous Gob, the, 112
Gashouse Gang, the, 148–50
Gateo, 31, 167
Geek, the, 66
Geep, the, xii
Generalissimo, 3
Gentleman, 85, 155
Georgia Deacon, the, 157
Georgi Boy, 159
Gerbil, the, 24–5
Gerbil, Jr., 25
Gerela's Guerillas, 33
Gipper, the, 144
Give 'em Hell, x
Glacier, the, 56
Glide, the, 148
Gnat, the, 156
Goat, the, 127
Godfather, the, 59
Godfather of Soul, the, x
Godzilla, 125
Goings, 169
Golden, the, 6
Golden Bear, the, 24
Golden Boy, 84
Golden Wheels, 41
Goldflinger, 9
Gomer, 69
Goober, 88
Good Doctor, the, 78
Good Evening, Mister, 5
Good Night, 155
Good Ol', 87
Goose, 146, 163
Gozzlehead, 65
Grandmaster Clash and the Furious Five, 155
Grand Orange, le, 89, 91
Gray Eagle, the, 162
Greasy, 176
Greasy Thumb, 158
Great, 6
Great, the, x
Greatest, the, 38
Great One, the, 168
Great Pumpkin, the 17
Great Right Hope, the, 19
Great White Hope, the, 134
Great White Shark, the, 133
Greco-, 6

Greek, the, 110
Greek Peak, the, 159
Greyhound, the, 27
Gruesome Twosome, the, 61
Guido, 68
Gumby, 138
Gump, 166
Guppy, 25

Hacksaw, 112
HacMan, 153
Half-Pint, 88
Halfway House, the, 86
Hammer, the, 112
Hands of Stone, 106
Happy, 105, 135
Hard Rock from Down Under, the, 111
Hari, 6
Harlem Coffee Cooler, the, 157
Harlem Spider, the, 157
Harvey's Wallbangers, 115
Hat, the, 85
Havana Bon Bon, 158
Hawk, 116
Hawk, the, 81
Hazel, 69
Heat, the, 119
Hecker the Wrecker, 84
Heinie, 135
Helicopter, the 126
Hello, 5
Herbie Lee, 94
Hercules, 137
Herkimer Hurricane, the, 156
Hewlett-Packard, 94
Hick from French Lick, the, 169
Hickie, 176
High, 6
High-Atolla of Slamola, the, 145
Highway Patrol Defense, 28
Hill, the, 122
Hillbilly, 122
Hippity, 88
Hippo, 27
His Accidency, x
His Fraudulency, x
His Rotundity, x
Hit 'Em Where They Ain't, 7
Hitman, 11
Hobble and Wobble, 120, 150
HoJo, 94
Holiday, 159
Hollywood, 159
Home Run, 110
Hondo, 107
Hooley, 138
Horribulls, the, 74
Horticulturist, the, 158
Hot, 14

Hot Rod, 49
House, 137
House that Ruth Built, the, 22
Hoya, 40
Hudson on the, 5
Huey, 41
Hulk, 69
Hulk Hogan, 101
Human, the, 34
Human Assist, the, 154
Human Eraser, the, 34
Human Freight Car, the, 34
Human Highlight Film, 34
Human Pencil in Sneakers, the, 174
Human Press, the, 154
Human Punching Bay, the, 34
Human Rain Delay, the, 34, 57
Human Scissors, the, 34
Human Skyscraper, the, 34
Human Windmill, the, 34
Hurt, the, 32

Ice, 51, 173
Ice Cube, the, 51, 156
Icebox, the, 119
Iceman, the, x, 51, 52
I Dub Thee, 6
Ike, x
Illinois Thunderbolt, the, 157
Imperial, 45
I Never Promised You a, 4
Innocent, the, 3
Invisi-, 86
ippiki okami, 167
Iron Butt, x
Ironhead, 102
Ironheart, 102
Iron Horse, the 102
Iron Mike, 102
Isaac, 68
Ivory Tower, the, 68
Izod, 3

Jack, x
Jaybird, 66
Jedge, 20
Jeep, 134
Jefferson St., 2
Jelly Roll, x
Jersey Bobcat, the, 157
Jersey Red, 158
Jo Jo, 105
Joltin', 142
Juice, 17
Juice, the 17
Jukebox Timebomb, ix
Jumbo, 135
Jump Steady, 67
Junior, 96, 132
Junkyard Dogs, the, 63

Kamikaze Kids, the, 141
Kangaroo Kid, the, 141

Kangaroosevelt, x
Kansas Rube, the 157
Kentucky Rosebud, the, 157
Kid, 20, 135, 143
Kid, the, 19–20
Kid Chocolate, 158
Kid Dropper, xi
Killer Bees, the, 63
Killer Tomatoes, the, 106
Kind John, 165
King, 135
Kingston, 4
Kitchen, the 118
Kitten, the, 23
Klinger, 69
Kong, 64
Kool FM, 105
K.T., 22

Large, 111
Larry, 28, 109
Last, the, 14
Launching Pad, the, ix, 11
Laverne and, 5
Lawrence Welk offense, the, 28
L.D., 22
Leave it To, 5
Lefty, ix, 56, 135, 169–70
Leiperville Shadow, the, 157
Lightning, 156
Lightning Rod, 50
Lip, the, 8, 150, 171
Little, xii
Little General, 173
Little Poison, 147
Little Train, 162
Livermore Larruper, the, 157
Load, 86,
Loco, 57
Lone Wolf, 167
Long, 91
Lord Charles, the, 45
Lo-rilla and Co-rilla, 120
Losing Pitcher, 9
Louie and Bouie Show, the, 120
Louisville Lip, the, 156
Louisville's Living Legend, the 78, 172
L.T., 22

M., 31
Mac the Sack, 63
MacFat, 72
Machine, the, 14
Machine Gun, xi
Macho, 85
Mad Bomber, the, 153
Mad Dawg, 64
Mad Dog, xi, 23
Mad Hungarian, the, 57
Mad Monk, the, 57
Mad Russian, the, 57
Mad Stork, the, 163
Magic, xi, 98, 99, 121
Magic Man, the, 101

Magic Markers, the, 107
Magnum, 5
Mailman, the, 52
Make Up, 6
Maltese, 5
Man, the, 43
Manassa Mauler, the, 141, 157
Manhattan Transfer, the, 156
Manila Gorilla, the, 38
Manly Marine, the, 112
Manos de Piedra, 106
Manster, 66
Manute Bol, 174
Man Who Ate Manhattan Beach, the, 72
Marino Corps, the, 33
Marks Brothers, the, 107
Marks of Excellence, 107
Martian, 125
Marvelous, 12, 155
Mascara, 29
Master Blaster, 171
Matchsticks, 173
McFilthy and McNasty, 151–153
McHale's Army, 33
Me, 171
Me and, 4
Mean, 61, 111, 170
Mean Green, the, 111
Meat Cleaver, 120
Men at, 4
Mendoza Line, the 96–7
Mercedes, 96
Merchant of Menace, the, 143
Mercury, 156
Mercury Swift, 37
Merry Mongoose, the, 141
Michael Jackson, 109
Michigan Assassin, the, 157
Mickey, 65, 135
Microwave, the, 119
Milkman, the, 166
Minnesota Fats, 158
Minnesota Gopher, 158
Miracle at Coogan's Bluff, the, 115–7
Missing Link, the, 101
Mister, 84
Mr. April, 84
Mr. Benny, 82
Mr. Bill, 86
Mr. Clutch, 169
Mr. Cub, 84
Mr. Ed, 84
Mr. Fuzzy, 84
Mr. Goodwrench, 82
Mr. Inside, 78
Mr. Monday, 84
Mr. October, 82
Mr. Outside, 6, 78, 82
Mr. Slambassador, 145
Mr. Wonderful, 101
Mrs. Butterworth, 82
Mitch the Stitch, 67

Moe, 109
Molester, the, 159
Monk, 145
Monkey Jesus, 3, 144
Monster, the 65
Monsters of the Midway, 141
Mookie, 14, 147
Moon Crater Face, 125
Moon Man, 57
Moose, 23, 40, 135
Mother, 6
Mother-in-Law Defense, the, 28
Mount, 14
Mouse, 3, 27, 86
Mouth that Roared, the, 159
Mudcat, 23
Muddy Waters, x
Muffin, 17
Mugger, the, 153
Muggsy, 154
Murderers' Row, 20
Murph the Surf, 41
Mute Rockne, 173
MX, 172

Nails, 113
Nebraska Wildcat, the, 157
Never Nervous, 173
Never Wrong, 172
New Dealer, the, x
Newsy, 47
New York Sack Exchange, the, 63
Night Train, 162
'Nique, 36
'Nique-a-Zoid, 36
No Bo, 122
No Name Defense, the, 63
No Neck, ix, 28
No Nose, xi
No Slack, 115
No Stars, 74
Noodles, 88
Nort, 69
'Nute Blockne, 173

O, 42
Octopus, the, 24
Ohio Fats, 24
Oil and, 3
Oil Can, ix, 132
Ol' Hopalong, 14
Ol' Perfesser, the, 115
Old 5-4-1, 170
Old Goat, 75
Old Second Inning, 101
Old Treetop, 148
Old Woman in the Red Cap, the, 174
Olive Head, 128
101 Strings
Onionhead, 29
Opie, 68
Orange Crush, the, 8, 63
Orchid Man, the, 111
Orville Moody, 132

Oscar, 147
Our 'Enery, 146
Over-the-Hill Gang, the, 150–1
Owl With out a Vowel, the, 31

Pags, 120
Paps, 132
Pea-Headed Giant, the, 29
Pea Ridge, 6
Pearl, 128, 171
Pearl, the, 128
Peddlin', 105
Pee Wee, 7
Peggy Lee, the, 45
Pele, 147
Pelusa, 38
Penguin, 75
Penitentiary Face, 153
Pepper, 2, 150
Perry, 5
Pete, 135
Philadelphia Dancing Master, the, 112
Philadelphia Pillies, the, 74
Philippine Gene, 158
Phi Slamna Jamma, 97
Piano, the, 117
Pillsbury Doughboy, the, 91
Pinky, 135
Pistol, 113
Pit Bull, 25
Pitchin' Mortician, the, 52
Pittsburgh Kid, the, 157
Please Come to, 4
Poison, 88
Pooh, 125
Pookie, 147
Poosh 'Em Up, 41
Pop, 130, 135
Popeye, 138
Pops, 17
Porky, 111
Possum Brothers, the, 25
Postage, 156
Pottawatomie Giant, the, 157
Prince, 4
Prince of Midair, the, 12
Private, 3
Psycho, 106
PT Boat, the, 155
Pudge, 72
Pueblo Fireman, the, 157
Puerto Rican Rolls-Royce, the, 96
Pulpwood, 167
Punch, 171
Purple, 3, 4
Purple People-Eaters, the, 63

Q, 42
Q Tip, 30
Quick, 170

Rabbit, 135
Radar, 113

Raf, 128
Raffles, 170
Rags and Pags, 120
Rainbow, 75, 171
Rambis Youth, 33
Rambo, 109
Rat, the, 24
Rats, 170
Raw Dealer, the, x
Razor, 30
Red, ix, 135–7, 165
Red Baron, 139
Refrigerator, the, 117
Rein, 6
Rembrandt, 37
Reno Rocket, the, 11
Rerun, 35
RFD, 5
Richter, 11
Rifle, the, 113
Rip, 135, 166
Ripper, 150
Rochedale Thunderbolt, the, 157
Rock, 162
Rocket, the, 91
Rocket Rod, 49–50
Rock Pile, the, 11
Rocky, 47–8, 108, 166
Rodney, 97
Rod Stupid, 137
Rolls, 3
Romancing the, 5
Roquette, le, 91
Roscommon Giant, the, 157
Round Mound of Rebound, the, 1, 72
Rowan and, 5
Rudy, 174
Rumble in the Jungle, ix, 38
Rush St., 2
Rusty, 89
Ryno, 75

Sack Dance, ix
Saginaw Kid, the, 157
St. Louis Louie, 158
St. Paul Cyclone, the, 157
St. Paul Phantom, the, 157
Salami, 5
Santo Clause, the, 56
Sarge, 75, 169
Sasquatch, 125
Satchel, 104
Satchmo, x
Satin, 3
Sawdust, 167
Say-Hey Kid, the, 36
Scarface, 120
Scoops, 44
Scooter, 147, 172
Scotch and, 5
Scotch Wop, the, 112
Scuffy, 44
Sea Cap, 144
Sean Cassidy Offense, 28
Senor Smoke, 168

Seoul Train, 159
Seven Blocks of Granite, the, 43
Sexy, 14
Shaker Mo, 167
Shaky, 75
Sheik, the, xii
Sheriff, 135
Sherwin Williams, 56
Shock Treatment, 85
Shoe, 169
Shoeless, 166
Shot, the, 113
Shotgun, 113
Shot Heard 'Round the World, the, 115–7
Shrine Game, 68
Sidecar, 126
Silent Force, the, 63
Silk, 19
Silk, the, 132
Singer Throwing Machine, the, 120
Singles, 5
Skates, 37
Skeets, 156
'Skew, 173
Slapsy, 85
Slats, 126
Sleepy, 105
Slick, 38
Slingin', 68
Sluggo, 138
Sly, 85
Smiley, 2
Smith Brothers, the, 29
Smokin' Joe, 38
Smurfs, the, 138–9
Snake, 23
Snap, 130
Socrates, 141
Sonar, 114
Sony, 94
SOS, 94
Souliers Blancs, 91
Soul Pole, the, 28
Space Cowboy, 56
Spaceman, 25, 56, 101
Sparky, 22, 50
Special K, 43
Spice, 2–3
Spiderman, 78
Splendid Splinter, the, 143
Spook, 166
Spoon, 2
Spud, 16–7, 150
Stan the Man Unusual, 57
Starvin', 173
Staten Island Scot, the, 117
Steel Curtain, 61
Steeplehead, 29
Stein, 78
Sterling Golden, 101
Stevie Wonder, 109
Sticks, 120
Stilt, the, 169

Stinky, 176
Stonefingers, 87
Stork, the, 162
Storm, 126
Strangler, 153
Subaru Staff, the, 91
Sudden, 75
Sugar, 47–8, 87, 108
Sugar Ray, 153
Sultan of Swat, the, 20
Sunoco, 96
Sunshine, 127
Super, 12
Superb, 173
Superbrat, 170
Super Red, 14
Supersub, 36
Surfin' U.S.A., 4
Surgeon, the, 81
Sweet, 14
Sweet 'n' Low, 47
Sweetness, 44
Sweetwater, 19
Swish, 47
Sydney Cornstalk, the, 157

T, 42, 166
Tackhammer, the, 182
Takin' Care of Business, 4
Tall Tactician, the, 126
Tall Tower of Gorgonzola, the, 112
Tallulah, 5
Tark the Shark, 25
Taters, 16
Tatu, 147
Teddy Ballgame, 143
10 . . . St., 3
Terminator, the, 134
Terre Haute Terror, the, 111
Terrible, the, x
Terrific, xii, 140
Tex, 100, 135, 150
Texas Strangers, the, 74
Three Finger, ix, 110, 171
Three Ninety-Five, 1
Three Stooges, the, 109
Thrilla in Manila, ix, 38
Throwin' Samoan, 124
Throwin' Swannanoan, 124
Thunderfoot, 89
Thunderpup, 75
Thurston B., 5
Timex, 96
Tin Man, the, 19
Tip, 124
Tipton Slasher, the, 157
Titanic, 125
Titlest Head, 94
Toast, 17
Toasted, 5
Toe, the, ix
Tonight, Let It Be, 5
Too Mean, 102
Tooter, 128
Toothless, 120

Tootsie, 128
Top Dawg, 64
Torn, 7
Tortilla Flats, 168
Touchdown Jesus, 145
Tough, xii
Toys in the Attic, 58
Traitor to His Class, a, x
Trash Can, 132
Tree, 148
Tricky Dick, x, 43
Triple Smart, 158
Troll, the, 64
Truth, the, 110, 170, 171
Tug, 124
Turk, the, 150
TWA, 69
Tway's Twoops, ix, 33
Twin Towers, the, 68, 94
Twirl, 12
Two-ton, 130

Uncle Charlie, the, 45
Union Gap, 4
Uriah, 4

Vaccine, 6
Vaulting Vicar, the, 140
Vincent Priceless, 108
Vincent Van Go, 37
Vinegar Bend, 156
Viqueens, the, 74
Vitalis, 38
Vodka, 5
Voice of God, the, 146
Vulture, the, 163

Wacko, 57
Wahoo, 168
Waldo, 31
Weasel, the, 42
Wee, 7
What the, 87
What's the Use?, 106
Wheeze Kids, the, 50
Whip, the, 166
White Magic, 99
White O., the, 125
White Rat, 133
White Shoes, 91
Whitey, 133, 135
Whizzer, 6
Whopper, the, 94
Wicks and Sticks, 120
Wide Load from Leeds, the, 72
Wild Bill, 150
Wild Bull of the Pampas, the, 85
Willie, 169
Wimp, 6
Wimpy, 138
Winds, 6
Wine, 5
Wizard of Oz, the, 19
Wobble, 120

Won't You Take Me on a
  Sea, 4
Woodchopper, the, 50
World, 173
World B., 12, 43
World Is My, the, 6
  Wrath of, 5
Wrong Way, 140

X, 42

Yak-Yak, 134
Yaz, 71
Yellow Pages, 91
Yogi, 176
Yom, 6
Yosemite Sam, 138
Young Again, 3

Z., 31
Zeke from Cabin Creek, 169

Ziggy, 91
Zippity, 87
Zoid, 34, 36

REAL NAMES

Aase, Don, 4
Abatemarco, Tom, 42–3
Abdul-Jabbar, Kareem, 101
Adams, Charles, 136
Adams, Franklin P., 74
Adams, John, x
Adams, Sherman, x
Addison, Rafael, 128
Adkins, Doug, 29
Aguirre, Mark, 9
Aikens, Willie, 134
Ainge, Danny, 117, 148, 174
Akerfelds, Darrel, 105
Akers, Fred, 28
Alexander, x
Alexander, Doyle, 5
Alexander, Hugh, 150
Ali, Muhammad, 38, 156
Allen, Alonza, 144
Allen, Eric, 156
Allen, Marcus, 101
Almon, Bill, 5
Altobelli, Joe, 127
Ambers, Lou, 156
Ames, Leon, 136
Anders, Benny, 97
Anderson, Arnold, 136
Anderson, George, 50, 171
Anderson, Ronald, 169
Andujar, Joaquin, 57
Antoinette, Marie, x
Aponte, Luis, 96
Arft, Henry, 87
Argyll Academy, 9
Armstrong, Louis, x
Asberry, Bryan, 109
Ashburn, Richie, 51
Askew, Vincent, 173
Attles, Al, 72
Austin, Clyde, 148
Ayala, Benny, 127

Babartsky, Al, 43
Backman, Wally, 4, 37
Bacon, Mary, 27
Badgro, Morris, 136
Baer, Max, 157
Bahr, Chris, 50
Bailey, Mark, 6
Baker, Frank, 110

Ballard, Jody, 96
Baller, Jay, 170
Bankhead, Scott, 5
Banks, Ernie, 82
Banks, Willie, 143
Bannon, Jimmy, 174
Baptiste, Brian, 7
Barbary, Donald, 136
Barber, Norwood, 7
Barber, Steve, 75
Barefield, Johnny, 78
Barkley, Charles, 72, 81
Barkley, John, 136
Barnes, Emile, 136
Barnes, Marvin, 47
Barnette, J.D., 50
Barr, Jim, 5
Barrett, Charles, 136
Barron, David, 135, 136
Basie, Count, x
Bass, Kevin, 97
Baugh, Larry, 87
Baugh, Sammy, 68
Baumer, Jim, 150
Baumgarten, Ross, 4
Baylor, Elgin, 37
Beatty, Warren, 148
Beck, Ed, 37
Beck, Walter, 89
Becker, Boris, 69, 139–40
Bedford, William, 173
Beet Diggers, 10
Belanger, Mark, 22
Belardi, Wayne, 176
Belicheck, Bill, 151
Bell, Gary, 168
Bell, James, 58
Benedict, Bruce, 5
Ben-Gals, 55
Bengough, Benny, 20
Bennett, James, 136
Benz, Amy, 96
Berlenbach, Paul, 157
Berman, Chris, 3–4, 82, 86,
  96
Berman, Len, 128
Bernhardt, Juan, 17
Bernstine, Nehames, 147
Berra, Lawrence Peter, 120,
  149, 176

Berry, Derek, 28
Berry, Tony, 28
Berry, Walter, 110–1
Bertania, Frank, 58
Bias, Len, 127
Bildilli, Emil, 122
Biletnikoff, Fred, 133
Bird, Doug, 162
Bird, James, 136
Bird, Larry, 81, 169
Bittman, Henry, 136
Blackwell, Ewell, 166
Blanchard, Felix, 78
Bleier, Adri, 48
Bleier, Robert, 48
Block, Billy, 105
Blount, Roy, Jr., 87
Blue, Vida, 60
Bluhm, Harvey, 136
Blyleven, Bert, 3, 158
Boggs, Wade, 5
Bogues, Tyrone, 154–5
Bohling, Brad, 105
Bol, Manute, 173–4
Bonk, Thomas, 97
Borom, Edward, 136
Boston, Daryl, 4
Boucher, Frank, 170
Bouie, Roosevelt, 120, 173
Bouton, Jim, 68
Bowa, Larry, 9, 75
Bowie, Anthony, 104
Bowser, James, 136
Boyd, Dennis, ix, 132
Bradley, Bill, 124–5
Bradshaw, Clyde, 148
Bradshaw, Terry, 15, 159
Bramble, Livingstone, 25
Branca, Ralph, 116
Branch, Norman, 136
Braun, Steve, 128
Brazile, Robert, 76
Breechen, Harry, 85
Brennan, Tom, 163
Brent, Eric, 125
Brett, George, 4, 76, 96
Breuer, Randy, 104
Bridges, Everett, 166
Brief, Anthony, 88
Bristol, Dave, 14

Broadbent, Harry, 171
Brock, Greg, 4
Bromwell, Perry, 156
Brosnan, Jim, 1
Broudy, Nathaniel, 143
Brown, Chris, 19
Brown, Darrell, 104
Brown, Helen Gurley, 171
Brown, Hubie, 36
Brown, James, 1
Brown, John, 136
Brown, Mordecai, ix, 110
Brown, Rickey, 82
Brown, Wiley, 172
Browning, Pete, 27
Brundage, Avery, 36
Bryant, Paul, 1, 60
Buck, Jack, 171
Buggs, Danny, 156
Bulldog Babes, 55
Bulldogettes, 52
Bumbry, Al, 27–8
Bumphus, Johnny, 85
Burke, Edmund, 1
Burt, Jim, 64
Burton, Richard, 143
Busby, Paul, 136
Butera, Lou, xi
Butler, Jerry, x
Byrd, Leroy, 36
Byrd, Sammy, 22

Camacho, Hector, 85
Camp, Howard, 136
Candiotti, Tom, 4
Canonero II, 142
Cardriche, Jaime, 117
Carew, Rod, 97
Carnera, Primo, 112
Carpentier, George, 111
Carr, M.L. 60
Carson, Bud, 61
Carson, Johnny, 117
Carter, Gary, 40
Carter, Jimmy, 99
Cartledge, Juvan, 7
Cartwright, Bill, 29, 86
Cary, Scott, 136
Castino, John, 4
Catholics, the, 144
Catledge, Terry, 93
Causey, Cecil, 136
Cauthen, Steve, 19–20
Cerdan, Marcel, 157
Cerone, Rick, 40
Cey, Ron, 4, 75
Chamberlain, Wilt, 126
Chance, Frank, 74
Chaney, Darrel, 69
Chant, Charlie, 60
Cheesemakers, 10
Chiesa, Gordon, 28
Chievous, Derrick, 30–1
Chiles, Pearce, 106
Chinks, the, 9
Christensen, Cuckoo, 144
Church, Emery, 168

Clark, Jack, 109
Clarke, Bobby, 24
Clayton, Mark, 107
Clemente, Roberto, 124, 168
Clifton, Nat, 19
Clyde, Benny, 148
Coffey, Jim, 157
Coghlan Eamonn, 44
Coleman, Clarence, 104
Coleman, Vince, 37
Coll, Vincent, xi
Collins, Dave, 5
Concepcion, Dave, 9
Conkwright, Allen, 136
Conn, Billy, 157
Connelly, John, 136
Conner, Lester, 151
Cook, Carroll, 31
Cooper Cecil, 115
Cooper, Henry, 146
Corbett, Jim, 85, 155
Cordero, Angel, 96
Cornjerkers, 10
Coryell, Don, 71
Corzine, Dave, 141
Costas, Bob, 91
Cotto, Henry, 5
Cotton Pickers, 10
Coulon, Johnny, 157
Counsilman, Doc, 1
Cowens, Al, 86
Cox, Danny, 25
Cox, Johnny, 37
Cox, Larry, 28
Craig, Frank, 157
Crawford, 168
Crigher, John, 37
Criminals, 10
Croce, Jim, 63
Cromartie, Cody Oh, 139
Cromartie, Warren, 139
Crook, Herb, 173
Crosby, Bing, x
Crowley, Tim, 144
Crum, Denny, 45
Cruz, Jose, 4
Cruz, Julio, 17
Cruz, Todd, 86, 109
Cunningham, Billy, 141

Dailey, Quintin, 42
Dale, Carroll, 112
Dallessandro, Dom, 142
Dauer, Rich, 57, 109
Daughters, Robert, 136
Davis, Charles, 39
Davis, George, 126
Davis, Glenn, 6, 82
Davis, Glenn (Mr. Outside),
   82
Davis, Harry, 176
Davis, Jody, 4, 75
Davis, Sam, 162
Davis, Sammy, Jr., 55
Davis, Walter, 27
Dawkins, Darryl, 89, 104, 105
Dawley, Bill, 5, 22

Day, Clyde, 6
Deal, Ellis F., 167
Dean, Jay, 149–50
Dean, Jerome, 149–50
Dena, Paul, 150
DeBartolo, Edward, 41
Dedmon, Jeff, 5
Deer, Rob, 6
De Gregorio, Ernie, 22, 43
DelGreco, Bobby, 110
De Los Angeles Rams,
   Maria, 67
Delucia, Fred, xi
DeMonner, Ron, 106
Dempsey, Jack, 141, 157
Dempsey, Rick, 109
Denny, John, 109
Dernier, Bob, 75
Desautels, Eugene, 136
Diaz, Bo, 122
Diaz, Mike, 122
DiBacco, Frank, 132
Dickerson, Eric, 82
Dickerson, Kevin, 85
Dickson, Paul, xi
DiMaggio, Joe, 142
Ditka, Mike, 102, 124
Dixon, Hanford, 24
Dolphin, Robert, 67
Donahue, Francis, 136
Donaldson, James, 104
Do Nascimento, Edson
   Arantes, 147
Dooin, Charles, 136
Doran, Bill, 4
Dots, 10
Downey, Alexander, 136
Downing, Brian, 3, 69
Downs, Jerome, 136
Dragons, the, 9
Drexler, Clyde, 148
Driesell, Charles, 169–70
Dropo, Walt, 23
Dryer, Fred, 61
Dubenion, Elbert, 41
Duck, Redonia, 165
Duda, Jacek, 87
Duda, Richie, 87
Dudek, Helmut, 89
Duhon, Brent, 94
Duliba, Bob, 87
Dundee, Johnny, 112
Dunkhorst, Ed, 34
Dunn, Jack, 20
Duper, Mark, 11, 107
Duran, Robert, 106
Durham, Hugh, 87
Durham, Leon, 75
Dunston, Shawon, 75
Durocher, Leo, 8, 149, 150
Durrett, Elmer, 136
Dykstra, Len, 113

Earnhardt, Dale, 102
Earnhardt, Ralph, 102
Easterly, Jamie, 6
Eaton, Zebulon, 136

Eckersley, Dennis, 56
Edgerton, Walter, 157
Edwards, Renard, 29
Ehret, Philip, 136
Eisenhower, Dwight, x
Ellington, Duke, x
Ellison, Pervis, 173
Elson, Bob, 71
Embraceable Ewes, the, 141
Embree, Charles, 136
Enatsu, Ytaku, 167
English, Alex, 122
Erving, Julius, 43, 76–78, 80, 149
Esiason, Norman, 89
Espinosa, Nino, 3
Estrada, Chuck, 75
Evans, Russell, 136
Evers, Johnny, 74
Ewing, Patrick, 40

Faber, Urban, 136
Facenda, John, 146
Falcone, Pete, 5
Farrell, Dick, 150
Farrell, Sean, 64
Ferguson, Bob, 14–5
Ferguson, John, 72
Ferns, Jim, 157
Ferrigno, Lou, 69
Fidrych, Mark, 163
Fighting Farmers, 10
Fine, Larry, 28
Fingers, Rollie, 30, 99
Finley, Charles O., 58–60
Finley, Chuck, 60
Firpo, Luis, 85
Fisher, Jack, 75
Fisher, John, 136
Fisk, Carlton, 72
Flaming Hearts, 10
Flannery, Tim, 109
Fletcher, Frank, 85
Flood, Paddy, 106–7
Flores, Chi Chi, 122
Flowers, Maureen, 7
Flowers, Tiger, 157
Floyd, Eric, 105
Flynn, Jim, 157
Foley, Jack, 113
Foli, Tim, 57
Forbes, Bold, 96
Ford, Betty, x
Forsch, Ken, 5
Foster, Rod, 49–50
Frame, Dave, 105
Franco, John, 68
Franco, Julio, 3, 5, 170
Frank, Tellis, 109
Fratello, Mike, 34–6
Frazier, Joe, 38
Frazier, Walt, 148
Free, Lloyd, 12, 43
Freeman, Marvin, 173
Frey, Jim, 44
Friend, Owen, 136

Frisch, Frankie, 150
Fuqua, John, 15, 134
Futch, Eddie, 38
Fykes, Dennis, 85

Gaines, Clarence, 147
Galento, Tony, 130
Gallon, Rickey, 45
Galloway, Jim, 47
Gant, John, 113
Gantner, Jim, 23, 69, 138
Gardner, Billy, 104
Garrett, Alvin, 139
Garvey, Steve, 138
Gaspar, Rod, 137
Gastineau, Mark, 63
Gault, Willie, 29
Gehrig, Lou, 102
Geiselmann, Gene, 25
Gentlemen, 155
Geoffrion, Bernie, 89
Gerela, Roy, 15, 33
Gergen, Joe, 170–1
Gervin, Derrick, 51
Gervin, George, 51
Gibbons, Mike, 157
Gilbert, Rod, 110
Giles, Bill, 150
Gilliam, Joe, 2
Gillingham, Gale, 112
Gilmore, Artis, 42
Gipp, George, 144
Gladden, Dan, 153
Gladding, Fred, 138
Glamack, George, 113–5
Gleason, Jackie, 158
Glouchkov, Georgi, 158–9
Godfrey, George, 84, 157
Golic, Bob, 64
Gooden, Dwight, 76, 78
Gorbachev, Mikhail, 133
Gore, Demetreus, 171
Gossage, Rich, 14, 56
Grange, Red, 141
Grant, Jim, 23
Greb, Harry, 34
Green, Dallas, 55
Green, Darrell, 172
Green Ted, 110
Greene, Joe, 61, 111
Greenwood, L.C., 61
Gregg, Eric, 55–6
Gregg, Randy, 76
Grier, Rosie, 61
Griffin, Alfredo, 3
Griffith, Darrell, 78, 172
Grim, Joe, 34
Groza, Lou, ix
Grubb, John, 4
Grunfeld, Ernie, 120
Guay, Paul, 82
Gullickson, Bill, 48
Gunkel, Woodward, 136
Gust, Ernest, 136
Guzman, Jose, 6
Gwosdz, Doug, 87

Haddix, Harvey, 23
Hagler, Marvin, 11–2
Hairston, Carl, 69
Hairston, Harold, 105
Hairston, Jerry, 138
Hall, Joe B., 17
Hampton, Dan, 64
Handy, Lynn, 76
Harge, Ira, 111
Hargis, John, 113
Hargrove, Mike, 34, 57
Harre, Rom, xii
Harris, Franco, 15
Harris, Harry, 34
Harrison, Longmire, 91
Harter, Dick, 141
Harvey, Greg, 125
Harvey, Paul, 150
Hassett, Joe, 113
Hatchets, 10
Hatton, Vernon, 37
Havlicek, John, 107
Hawkins, Connie, 81
Hawkings, Elvin, 42
Hayes, Rutherford B., x
Hayes, Von, 4, 170
Haywood, Spencer, 28
Hayworth, Myron, 136
Hazzard, Walt, 124
Hearns, Thomas, 11
Heath, Mike, 5
Hecker, Charles, 84
Hedberg, Anders, 138
Heeney, Tom, 111
Heep, Danny, 4
Heinsohn, Tom, 81
Henderson, Thomas, 159
Hendricks, Ted, 163
Henke, Tom, 51
Herr, Tommy, 5
Herring, Arthur, 135, 136
Herzog, Dorrel Norman, 3, 37, 133
Heyward, Craig, 152
Hicks, Dwight, 150
Hill, Clifford, 136
Hill, Rod, 68
Hill, Sam, 87
Hillerich, Bud, 27
Hinault, Bernard, 11
Hirsch, Elroy, 67
Hitchcock, Billy, 147
Hitten, Chip, 1
Hittle, Lloyd, 136
Hodges, Russ, 115
Hoff, Chester, 136
Hoffman, Clarence, 136
Holmes, Baskerville, 173
Holmes, Ernie, 61
Holmes, Larry, 96
Holt, James, 136
Hoover, J. Edgar, xi
Hope, Bob, 24
Hope, Bob (the other one), 144
Hopp, Johnny, 88
Houston, Kevin, 23

Houston Gamblers, 41
Howard, Regina, 120
Howe, Art, 6, 40
Howell, Jay, 5
Howell, Murray, 136
Hoy, William, 167
Hoyt, Waite, 52
Hrabosky, Al, 57
Hubbard, Glenn, 138
Hudkins, Ace, 157
Hundley, Rod, 48–9
Hunt, Lamar, ix
Hunter, Jim, 60
Hunter, Leslie, 101
Hurdle, Clint, 69

Immaculate Reception, the, 15
Ireland, Tim, 57
Ivan, x
Ivy, Hercle, 88

Jackson, Andrew, 171
Jackson, Jackie, 126
Jackson, Joe, 166
Jackson, Reggie, 82
Jacobs, Forrest V., 166
James, Bill, 22
James, Bob, 6
James, Frank, 2
James, Karl Frank, 2, 125
James, Lionel, 162
Janes, 55
Jeffires, James, 134
Jenkins, Ferguson, 24–5
Jennings, Bubba, 168
Jennings, Hugh, 174
Jet Pilot, 105
Johannson, Ingemar, 146
Johnson, Billy, 91
Johnson, Butch, 69
Johnson, Cecil, 125
Johnson, Cliff, 4
Johnson, Dennis, 81
Johnson, Earvin, xi, 39, 98
Johnson, Henry, 34
Johnson, Hernell, 134
Johnson, Howard, 94
Johnson, Jack, 134, 157
Johnson, Kannard, 109
Johnson, Lynbert, 88
Johnson, Lyndon, 171
Johnson, Reggie, 141
Johnson, Thomas, 2
Johnson, Vance, 64
Johnson, Vinnie, 117
Johnson, Walter, 162
Johnston, Wilfred, 136
Johnstone, Jay, 27
Jones, Deacon, 61
Jones, Keith, 115
Jones, Maurice, 136
Jones, Rupert, 4
Jones, Shelton, 106
Jones, Steve, 47
Jordan, Michael, 132

Juelich, John, 136
Jurgensen, Sonny, 120

Kalis, Todd, 94
Kaplan, Nathan, xi
Katz, Joel, 127
Kazmierzak, Edward, 145
Keeler, Willie, 7
Kellett, Donald, 136
Kelley, Rich, 94
Kelly, George, xi
Kelly, Tommy, 157
Kemp, Jack 41
Kennedy, Darryl, 104, 125
Kennedy, John, 56
Kennedy, John F., x, 171
Kennedy, Pat, 7
Kennedy, Terry, 132
Kepshire, Kurt, 25
Ker, Crawford, 109
Ketchel, Stanley, 157
Killefer, Wade, 136
Kilmer, Billy, 120, 150
Kilpatrick, Spious, 2
Kim, Duk Koo, 165
Kinchen, James, 119
King, Albert, 56
King, Bernard, 120
King, Don, 38
King, Larry, 43
Kingdom, Roger, 50
Kingman, Dave, 64
Kinsella, Robert, 136
Kipper, Bob, 6
Kison, Bruce, 6
Kleinow, John, 136
Klier, Leo, 87
Kluless, Ted, 103
Klutts, Mickey, 72
Knight, Ray, 6
Knotts, Don, 69
Knowings, Herman, 126–7
Knox, Chuck, 71
Koch, Bill, 12
Koch, Frederick, 12
Koncak, Jon, 19
Kreitz, Ralph, 136
Kress, Ralph, 136
Kroc, Joan, 132
Kroc, Roy, 132
Krzyzewski, Mike, 42
Kubek, Tony, 106
Kuenn, Harvey, 115
Kuhn, Walter, 136
Kurland, Bob, 168
Kuzaba, Bob, 133

Lacheman, Rene, 59–60, 86, 109, 151
LaCoss, Mike, 3, 44
LaCoste, Rene, 23
Ladies, 55
Lady Friars, 55
Lady Gamecocks, 55
Lady Statesmen, 55
Lahti, Jeff, 5

Laimbeer, Bill, 153
Lalonde, Edouard, 47
Lamonica, Daryle, 153
LaMotta, Jake, 47, 157
Landenberger, Kenneth, 136
Landreaux, Ken, 22
Landry, Tom, 9
Lane, Dick, 162
Lang, Jack, 140
Langford, Sam, 157
Larkin, Tippy, 157
Lary, Frank, 16
Lasorda, Tommy, 58, 138
Lau, Charlie, 76, 138
Lavagetto, Harry, 147
Lavigne, George, 157
Layden, Elmer, 144
Layden, Frank, 120
Lazzeri, Tony, 41
Lee Bill, 25, 56, 101
Lee, Eun Jung, 159
Lehrer, Jim, 168
Leibrandt, Charlie, 37
LeMond, Greg, 11
Leonard, Jeff, 153
Leonard, Ray, 47
Lever, Lafayette, 72
Levingston, Cliff, 137
Lewis, Ed, 153
Lewis, Emmanuel, 34
Lewis, Ernie, 130
Lieb, Fred, 22
Lincicome, Bernie, 41
Linseman, Ken, 24
Lipps, Louis, 14
Lipscomb, Eugene, 58
Liston, Sonny, 1
Littell, Mark, 57
Littler, Gene, 14
Lloyd, Lewis, 99–101
Logan, Dave, 125
Lohaus, Brad, 20
Lom, Benny, 140
Lombardi, Vince, 43
Long, Howie, 12
Long, Nelson, 136
Lopez, Al, 71
Lopez, Aurelio, 168
Los Angeles, Clippers, 86
Los Angeles Dodgers, 85
Los Angeles Lakers, 85
Los Angeles Raiders, 86
Los Angeles Rams, 86
Lott, Ronnie, 150
Loughran, Tommy, 112
Louis, Joe, 8, 85
Louisville Slugger, 27
Lowenstein, John, 5, 97
Lucas, Charles, 136
Lucas, John, 105
Lumberjacks, 55
Lumberjills, 55
Lundry, Laram, 61
Lutz, Louis, 136
Luvabulls, the, 74
Lyle, Albert, 22

Lynn, Japhet, 136
Lyons, Steve, 106
Lysander, Rick, 3

M., Frankie, 30
M., Zenon, 31
McAdoo, Bob, 28
McAvoy, Jock, 157
McCaffery, Fran, 99
McCammon, Bob, 138
McCarver, Tim, 101
McCatty, Steve, 107
McClannahan, Rob, 138
McCray, Carlton, 172
McDaniel, Xavier, 42
McDermott, Frank, 136
McDowell, Oddibe, 3
McDowell, Sam, 75
McEnroe, John, Jr., 132
McEnroe, John, Sr., 132
McFadden, Ken, 3, 27
McGee, Tony, 63
McGee, Willy, 4
McGill, Bill, 122
McGillicuddy, Cornelius, 1, 126
McGraw, Frank, 45, 124
McGuire, Al, 148
McGuire, Dick, 43
McGurn, Jack, xi
McHale, Kevin, 33, 174
Mack, Connie, 1, 126
McKee, Ray, 136
McLaughlin, Joe, 64
Maclean, Paul, 72
McLish, Calvin, 121
McMahon, Jim, 102, 132
McManus, Jack, xi
McNally, Art, 15
McNeal, Gerald, 156
MacNeill, Robin, 68
McQueen, Cozell, 120
McQuillen, Glenn, 136
Macy, Kyle, 38
Madden, John, 117
Madison, James, 171
Madlock, Bill, 29
Maglie, Sal, 50–1
Mahorn, Rick, 151, 153
Maier, Henry, 102
Majerus, Rick, 80
Malamud, Bernard, 27
Maler, Jim, 138
Malone, Jeff, 174
Malone, Karl, 52
Malone, Moses, 105, 166
Mancini, Ray, 165
Manigault, Earl, 127
Man o' War, 14
Maradona, Diego, 38
Maravich, Pete, 113
Marciano, Rocky, 47–8, 157
Marcos, Ferdinand, 133
Marfa, 153
Marino, Dan, 33
Marion, John, 136

Marion, Marty, 24
Martin, Alfred, 36
Martin, Charles, 102
Martin, Clarence, 109
Martin, Jerry, 5
Martin, Richard, 110
Mason, Mike 5
Mata, Victor, 6
Mathers, Jerry, 23
Mathewson, Christy, 40–1
Matthews, Gary, 75
Mauch, Gene, 132
May, Milt, 138
Mayberry, John, 5
Maxwell, Cedric, 19
Meany, Tom, 149
Mecklenburg, Karl, 27
Meddlin, Jay, 105
Mcdich, George, 76
Medwick, Joe, 163
Melvin, Bob, 4
Mendoze, Mario, 96–7
Merrill, Casey, 64
Messersmith, Andy, 66
Meyer, Jack, 150
Meyer, Russ, 57
Middleton, Frankie, 31
Mikan, George, 168
Mikita, Stan, 85
Milinichik, Joe, 118
Miller, Cheryl, 108
Miller, Don, 144
Miller, Leo, 136
Miller, Reggie, 108
Minton, Greg, 57
Mitchell, Mike, 67
Mizell, Wilmer, 156
Mlkvy, Bill, 31
Moley, Kevin, 106
Molina, Scott, 134
Molloy, Edward, 145
Monroe, Earl, 120
Monroe, Marilyn, 142
Montana, Joe, 145
Montefusco, John, 19
Moody, Orville, 169
Moore, Archie, 141
Moore, Donnie, 56, 135
Moore, Lloyd, 86–7
Moore, Pearl, 128
Moreland, Keith, 75
Moret, Roger, 66
Morgan, James, 136
Morgan, Joe, 50
Morganfield, McKinley, ix
Morris, Eugene, 156
Morris, Jack, 14
Morton, Ferdinand, x
Moseby, Lloyd, 167
Moskau, Paul, 5
Most, Johnny, 153
Mountaindears, 55
Mountaineers, 55
Muhammad, Calvin, 94
Mulcahy, Hugh, 9
Munger, George, 136

Munson, Clarence, 137
Murff, John, 137
Murphy, Swayne, 69
Murphy, Jack, 41
Murray, John, 137
Musial, Stan, 43
Musil, Frantisek, 87
Mussolini, Benito, 40

Namath, Joe, 2
Nance, Larry, 145
Neal, Fred, 38
Neale, Alfred, 176
Nehemiah, Renaldo, 156
Nekola, Francis, 174
Nelson, Don, 34
Newton, Nate, 118–9
Newton, Tim, 119
Nichols, Reid, 6
Nicholson, Bill, 47
Nicklaus, Jack, 24
Niekro, Phil, 58
Nixon, Norm, 43
Nixon, Richard, x
Nonnenkamp, Leo, 137
Norman, Greg, 133
Notre Dame, 144–5
Novikoff, Lou, 57
Nunez, Tommy, 29

O'Brien, Ralph, 115
Odom, John, 59
O'Dowd, Mike, 157
Oh, Saduharu, 139
Ojeda, Bob, 45
Okorodudu, Abraham, 78
Olajide, Michael, 132
Olajuwon, Akeem, 68, 91
Olberding, Mark, 141
Oldham, John, 137
Oliver, Al, 44
Oliver, Edward, 111
Olsen, Merlink 61
O'Neal, Tatum, 101
O'Neill, James, 124
O'Neill, Thomas, 124
Orr, Bobby, 110
Orr, Louis, 120, 173
Osceola Astros, 41
Osteen, Claude, 69
Ostergard, Roberts, 137
Ott, Ed, 64
Owen, Spike, 171
Owens, Jim, 150
Owens, Paul, 150
Owens, Thomas, 137

Pabor, Charles, 174
Pacheco, Ferdie, 76
Paciorek, Tom, 138
Paddio, Gerald, 87
Padgett, Ernest, 137
Pagliarulo, Mike, 120
Paige, Arnold, 32
Paige, Leroy, 104
Palmer, Jim, 17, 126, 132

Palmer, Paul, 9
Papke, Billy, 157
Pappas, Milt, 75
Parish, Robert, 139
Parker, Charlie, x
Patterson, Elvis, 17
Patterson, Floyd, 37
Paultz, Billy, 94
Pavelich, Mark 52, 138
Payton, Walter, 44
Pearson, Barry, 15
Pekin High, 9
Pena, Tony, 5, 167
Perez, Tony, 50
Pericles, 29
Perrault, Gilbert, 110
Perry, Gaylord, 75, 86
Perry, William, 117, 118
Pesky, Johnny, 115
Petersen, Jim 68
Petri, Julius, 96
Petrolle, Billy, 111, 157
Pezzuoli, Dave, 56
Phelps, Ken, 5
Phelps, Richard, 145
Phillips, Clarence, 137
Phillips, Oail Andrews, 1
Pittman, Joe, 6
Pittsburgh Maulers, 41
Plank, Doug, 124
Poca Dots, 10
Poole, Bryant, 60
Powell, John, 137
Price, Joe, 3
Price, Sloan, 165
Professional Bowlers
  Association, 105
Puckett, Kirby, 4
Puddy, Glenn, 126
Puleo, Charlie, 6
Pulford, Bob, 173
Pyle, C.C., 140

Qawi, Dwight, 157
Quick, Lyman, 2
Quirk, Jamie, 4
Quisenberry, Dan, 45, 159

Radatz, Dick, 65–6
Raines, Tim, 3, 30
Rambelles, 55
Rambis, Kurt, 33
Ramirez, Mario, 68
Ramos, Sugar, 47
Rams, 55
Ransey, Kelvin, 82
Rattlerettes, 52
Rawlings, John, 137
Rayl, Jimmy, 34
Reagan, Ronald, 132
Reardon, Jeff, 134
Red Elephants, 10
Redford, Robert, 27
Redus. Gary, 6
Reese, Harold, 7
Regan, Phil, 163

Reigels, Roy, 140
Rembert, Larry, 82
Repulski, Eldon, 166
Retton, Mary Lou, 117
Reuss, Jerry, 3, 30
Reyes, Gilberto, 29
Reynolds, Jack, 112
Rice, Grantland, 141, 144
Richard, Maurice, 91
Richards, Bob, 140
Richards, Golden, 41
Richardson, Jerome, 104, 125
Richardson, Micheal Ray,
  48, 105
Richmond, Mitch, 170
Righetti, Dave, 4, 120
Rijo, Jose, 3
Ripley, Allen, 45
Risko, Johnny, 157
Rivers, Glenn, 80, 105
Rivers, Mickey, 65
Rizzuto, Phil, 147
Roberts, Charles, 137
Roberts, Glenn, 106
Roberts, Rene, 110
Robertson, Oscar, 42
Robinson, Cliff, 148
Robinson, Frank, 137
Robinson, Jackie, 68, 109
Robinson, Len, 27
Robinson, Ray, 47
Roche, John, 137
Rockne, Knute, 144
Rodriguez, Juan, 122–4
Rogers, Kenny, 41
Rohler, Curv, 105
Rolfe, Robert, 137
Rollings, William, 137
Rollins, Wayne, 148
Romanick, Ron, 6
Roosevelt, Franklin, x
Rose, Pete, 9, 50, 68, 94,
  131, 150
Rosenbloom, Maxie, 85
Rouse, Curtis, 104
Royster, Jerry, 6, 66
Ruffings, Charles, 137
Ruhle, Vern, 6
Ruland, Jeff, 151
Rupp, Adolph, 37
Ruth, George Herman, 20,
  27, 41, 149
Ryan, Buddy, 117, 124
Rye, Eugene, 88

Sabonis, Arvidis, 96
St. Clair, Bob, 66
Salk, Jonas, 31
Salters, Ray, 109
Sample, Billy, 3, 165
Sampson, Ralph, 68, 91
Sandberg, Ryne, 75
Sanders, Eugene, 125
Sanderson, Winfrey, 6
Sann Dave, 84
Santana, Rafael, 98–9

Santo, Ron, 56
Sardinias, Eligio, 158
Saunders, Phil, 50
Sax, Steve, 58, 109
Scales, DeWayne, 11
Schillings, Elbert, 137
Schmeling, Max, 85
Schmidt, Mike, 94
Schoendienst, Albert, 137
Schofield, Dick, 163, 165
Schofield, Dicky, 165
Schuh, Randy, 5
Schulian, John, 170, 171
Schultz, Dave, 112
Schwarzenegger, Arnold, 134
Scott, Mike, 6, 44
Sea Gulls, 55
Seattle Slew, 41
Seattle SuperSonics, 86
Seaver, Tom, 5, 140
Seay, Virgil, 139
Secretariat, 14
Seikaly, Rony, 159
Sellers, Jeff, 5
Sellers, Peter, 81
Sewell, Rip, 45
Shannon, Maurice, 137
Sharkey, Jack, 112
Sheets, Ben, 162
Sheets, Larry, 3
She Gulls, 55
Shepherd, Jeff, 3, 144
Sheridan, Eugene, 137
Shines, Anthony, 30
Shirley, Bob, 5
Shoemaker, William, 169
Shugrue, Young, 157
Siegle, Tony, 109, 150
Sierra, Reuben, 6
Silas, James, 151
Simmons, Ted, 30
Simpson, Orenthal James, 17
Sinatra, Frank, x
Singer, Bill, 120
Skipper, James, 135
Skowron, Bill, 40
Slavin, Frank, 157
Smith, Adrian, 37
Smith, Andre, 167
Smith, Bubba, 169
Smith, Derek, 172
Smith, James, 85
Smith, Jeff, 157
Smith, Kate, 171
Smith, Lonnie, 37
Smith, Lou, 48
Smith, Marvin, 137
Smith, Noland, 156
Smith, Ozzie, 19, 163
Smith, Pat, 81
Smith, Reginald, 138
Smith, Ted, 110
Smith, Willard, 137
Smyth, James, 137
Snell, Ray, 125
Snipes, Renaldo, 84

Socks, 9
Soto, Mario, 5
Speaker, Trio, 162
Speier, Chris, 6
Spencer-Devlin, Helen, 17
Spielberg, Steven, 106
Spinks, Leon, 48
Springsteen, Bruce, x
Staak, Bob, 52
Stabler, Ken, 23
Stabley, Fred, 98
Stagg, Amos Alonzo, 141
Stallcup, Thomas, 137
Stallone, Sylvester, 48, 85, 108
Stallworth, Aubrey, 29
Stamps, Sylvester, 156
Stanhouse, Don, 57
Stargell, Willie, 17
Staub, Daniel, 69, 89–91
Steinbrenner, George, 58
Steiner, James, 137
Steinman, Sam, 20
Stengel, Charles, 115
Stenhouse, Mike, 94
Steppe, Brook, 84
Stewart, Sammy, 124
Stingley, Darryl, 153
Stinson, Marvin, 84
Stoddard, Tim, 40
Stone, George, 113
Street, Charles, 150
Strickland, Rod, 50
Strickland, Roger, 113
Strickler, George, 144
Strike, Dale, 105
Stroughter, Steve, 109
Stuart, Dick, 81
Stuhldreher, Harry, 144
Sullivan, John L., 157
Summer, John, 85
Swain, Gary, 29
Swearingen, Fred, 15
Sweat, Ed, 14

Tanana, Frank, 5
Tapscott, Ed, 91
Tarkanian, Jerry, 25
Tarzans, 55
Tatum, Jack 15, 153
Tatum, Reece, 163
Tavares, Frank, 158
Taylor, Bud, 111
Taylor, Elizabeth, 143, 171
Taylor, Lawrence, 22
Taylor, Roland, 78
Templeton, Garry, 67
Testaverde, Vinnie, 108
Theodore, George, 162
Theus, Reggie, 2
Thomas, Gorman, 138
Thomas, Robert, 137
Thompson, Alvin, 125
Thompson, Billy, 173
Thompson, Broderick, 109
Thompson, George, 81

Thompson, Jack, 124
Thompson, John, 155
Thompson, Mychal, 82
Thomson, Bobby, 116–7
Throneberry, Marv, 155
Thurmond, Mark, 68
Tigers, 55
Tigerettes, 55
Tillis, James, 170
Tinker, Joe, 74
Tiriac, Ion, 140
Tittle, Y.A., 162
Tobin, Jim, 174
Tolstoy, Leo, 171
Toney, Andrew, 151
Torphy, Walter, 137
Tracey, Tom, 134
Tramback, Stephen, 137
Treadway, Thadford, 137
Trillo, Manny, 4, 170
Trojans, 55
Trojanes, 55
Troup, John, 25
Trout, Paul, 172
Trout, Steve, 75, 171–2
Trucks, Virgil, 88
Trueblood, Zack, 115
Truman, Harry, x
Tudor, John, 3
Tunney, Gene, 112
Turgeon, Mark, 81
Turner, Andrew, 173
Turner, Ted, 66, 136, 139
Turner, Tina, 171
Turpin, Melvin, 17
Tway, Bob, 33, 94
Tyler, John, x
Tyler, Terry, 42

Utah Jazz, 86
Uzcudun, Paulino, 111–2

Vadnais, Carol, 110
Valachi, Joe, xi
Valenzuela, Fernando, 45, 168
Valvano, Jim, 42
Van Robays, Maurice, 45
Vaughan, Jim, 27
Veal, Orville, 167
Venable, Max, 97
Viola, Frank, 4
Vitale, Dick, 39
Vukovich, George, 170

Wade, Erskine, 165
Wagner, Milton, 173
Walcott, Joe, 157
Walker, Clarence, 143
Walker, Dixie, 85
Walker, Fred, 68
Walker, Harry, 85
Walker, Jerry, 75
Waller, John, 137
Walton, Bill, 98
Walton, Danny, 138

Walton, Mike, 75
Wanderone, Rudolf, 158
Waner, Lloyd, 147
Waner, Paul, 147
Ward, Jeff, 36
Ward, Joe, 29
Warner, Pop, 1
Washington, Dwayne, 128
Washington, George, 20, 171
Waters, Bucky, 36
Watson, Tom, 99
Watts, Slick, 38
Weaver, Earl, 40, 57
Weaver, Eddie, 120
Weaver, Mike, 137
Webb, Anthony, 16
Webb, Samuel, 137
Webster, Marvin, 34
Welch, Bob, 4
Welch, Frank, 176
Welk, Ike, 157
Wells, Warren, 153
Wert, Don, 87
West, Jerry, 169
White, Byron, 6
White, Dwight, 61
White, Joseph, 105
White, Randy, 66, 118
Wicks, Sue, 120
Wilkes, Keith, 19
Wilkins, Dominique, 34–6
Willard, Gerry, 170
Willard, Jess, 157
Williams, Carl, 170, 171
Williams, Chip, 74
Williams, Donald, 165
Williams, James, 25
Williams, Reggie, 8
Williams, Stan, 32
Williams, Steve, 76
Williams, Ted, 143
Williams, Terry, 22
Williams, Vanessa, 171
Williams, Walt, ix, 28
Williamson, Carlton, 150
Williamson, Fred, 112
Wilson, Bert, 142
Wilson, George, 176
Wilson, Glenn, 4, 122
Wilson, Robert, 137
Wilson, Tony, 69
Wilson, Willie (Mookie), 14, 147
Wilson, Willie, 137
Wine, Bobby, 150
Wingo, Absalom, 137
Winkler, Henry, 133
Wise, Rick, 24
Wojciechowitz, Alex, 43
Womack, Horace, 174
Woolf, George, 52
Woolridge, Orlando, 42
Word, Barry, 14
Worsley, Lorne, 166
Worthington, Al, 137
Worthington, Robert, 137

Wothke, Les, 23
Wright, Charles, 155
Wright, Eric, 150
Wright, Poncho, 172
Wright, Pop, 99
Wynegar, Butch, 3
Wynn, Early, 71, 110

Yanger, Benny, 157
Yankee Stadium, 22

Yastrzemski, Carl, 71, 143
Youmans, Floyd, 45
Young, Denton, 126
Youngblood, Jack, 61
Youngblood, Joel, 4

Zahn, Geoff, 5, 84
Zamboni, the, 52
Zimmer, Don, 24–5
Zimmer, Tom, 25

Zisk, Richie, 145
Zivojinovic, Slobodan, 140
Zoeller, Frank, 97
Zuber, Bill, 88
Zupo, Frank, 88